cook

cook

VISUALIZE THE
PERFECT PLATE

·······································

*A photographic guide
to cooking from scratch*

Bath · New York · Cologne · Melbourne · Delhi
Hong Kong · Shenzhen · Singapore · Amsterdam

This edition published by Parragon Books Ltd in 2016 and distributed by

Parragon Inc.
440 Park Avenue South, 13th Floor
New York, NY 10016
www.parragon.com

Copyright © Parragon Books Ltd 2012–2016

Cover design by Karli Skelton
Cover photography by Max and Liz Haarala Hamilton
Cover food styling by Sara Lewis
Photography by Mike Cooper
Home economy by Lincoln Jefferson
Internal design by Talking Design
Introduction by Linda Doeser

All rights reserved. No part of this publication may be reproduced, stored in a retrieval system, or transmitted, in any form or by any means, electronic, mechanical, photocopying, recording, or otherwise, without the prior permission of the copyright holder.

ISBN 978-1-4723-9322-7

Printed in China

Notes for the Reader
This book uses standard kitchen measuring spoons and cups. All spoon and cup measurements are level unless otherwise indicated. Unless otherwise stated, milk is assumed to be whole, eggs are large, individual fruits and vegetables are medium, pepper is freshly ground black pepper, and salt is table salt. Unless otherwise stated, all root vegetables should be peeled prior to using.

The times given are an approximate guide only. Preparation times differ according to the techniques used by different people, and the cooking times may also vary from those given.

For best results, use a food thermometer when cooking meat. Check the latest government guidelines for current advice.

contents

This superb cookbook, richly packed with wonderful and particularly useful photographs, will prove to be an invaluable and fascinating addition to any cook's bookshelf. The recipes are clear, easy to follow, beautifully illustrated, and temptingly tasty, so whatever your level of expertise in the kitchen, you are virtually guaranteed success every time.

Every recipe starts with a photograph of all the ingredients, but this is more than just a pretty picture or—even less useful—a montage that is not to scale, so that an orange segment appears the same size as a duck breast. Instead, it serves as an at-a-glance check that you have everything ready before you start cooking. Simply comparing the picture with the ingredients arranged on your own countertop will help you be sure that you haven't forgotten anything and, when it's time to stir in the herbs, for example, you've already chopped them as specified in the ingredients list. If you're not sure how thinly to slice lemongrass or how golden toasted nuts should be, a glance at the photograph will provide an instant answer.

Every short and straightforward step of the method is clearly explained without any jargon or incomprehensible technical terms. Once again, what you see in the photograph is what you should expect to see in your own kitchen. Not only is this reassuring for the beginner, but those with more experience will find it a helpful reminder of the little touches and tricks that can easily be overlooked. Each recipe ends with a mouthwatering photograph of the finished dish, complete with any serving suggestions where relevant.

Why you need this book
This book is the complete answer to the perennial question, "What shall I cook today?," because it is packed with delicious fuss-free recipes for all occasions, seasons, and tastes. Whether you want to rustle up a quick midweek family dinner, create a special meal for guests, prepare a healthy snack, bake an afternoon treat, or try your hand at something a little more exotic than usual, you are sure to find just the recipes you want. And whether you're a complete novice or a more experienced cook, you're sure of success on a plate.

Buying fresh ingredients

> Not only is local seasonal produce less expensive, but because it hasn't had to travel a long distance, it will have a better flavor, texture, and color and retain a higher level of nutrients. Imported fruits and vegetables are often disappointing.

> Root vegetables should be firm with no damp patches. Tomatoes and bell peppers should have shiny, taut skins. Avoid leafy vegetables with slimy, wilting, yellowing, or discolored leaves. Green beans should be crisp enough to snap if you bend them.

> In general, fruit that looks heavy for its size, is firm, and unwrinkled will be fresh. Soft fruits, such as nectarines, should look dry and plump with no signs of mold or wetness. A ripe melon and pineapple should smell fragrant and give slightly when gently pressed.

> Look for fish with a firm body, tight-fitting scales, unfading colors, red gills, and full, bright eyes. It should have a pleasant, not fishy smell. Fish and

shellfish deteriorate rapidly so are best eaten on the day of purchase, but they can be kept in the refrigerator for 1 day.

> Meat and poultry should look appetizing and smell pleasant. Depending on the type of meat, the color will be in the pale pink to red range; it should never look gray. Remember that good-quality mature beef is a dull, dark red. Any fat should be creamy white, not yellow, and waxy, not slimy.

> Keep an eye on the expiration dates on dairy produce, eggs, and processed meats.

Useful pantry standbys

Canned goods Canned tomatoes feature in many recipes from casseroles to pasta sauces and are often a much better option than fresh ones, especially out of season or during a poor summer. Canned legumes, such as chickpeas and beans, are convenient but more expensive than dried legumes, which require overnight soaking and long cooking.

Dried pasta is the busy cook's best friend. It has a very long shelf life and takes little time to cook. It is, therefore, a good idea to have a selection of different shapes, including penne, and at least one long type, such as spaghetti or tagliatelle.

Flour All-purpose flour is used for all kinds of purposes: making pastry, mixing pancakes, thickening sauces. It is also used for cakes, cookies, and dumplings. If you have self-rising flour, you can use it as a substitute in the latter group by reducing the baking powder by 1½ teaspoons for every 1 cup of flour and any salt by ⅛ teaspoon per cup of flour. However, it is better to use the flour recommended in the recipe.

Herbs and spices Fresh herbs are almost always more aromatic and flavorsome than dried, and some delicate herbs, such as parsley and basil, are better fresh than dried. However a stock of more robust dried herbs, such as rosemary and bay leaves, is invaluable. Buy both dried herbs and ground spices in small quantities because they quickly lose their aroma and flavor. Store for up to three months in a cool, dark place. Cardamom, coriander, cumin, fennel seeds, and peppercorns are best bought whole and freshly ground when needed and they also last a little longer.

Oils Olive oil is full of flavor and ideal for salad dressings and special dishes. It is expensive, so choose a cheaper bland type, such as sunflower or peanut, for everyday cooking. Store in a cool, dark place to prevent oils from turning rancid. Don't spend money on expensive nut oils if you plan to use them only once.

Rice Long-grain rice is a useful staple. However, if you want to make a successful risotto, you will need an Italian rice, such as Arborio or other type of risotto rice.

Vinegar White wine vinegar is a useful all-round ingredient. Red wine and cider vinegar are also multipurpose. Balsamic vinegar, which is now a fashionable choice, is much more expensive and should be used sparingly. You can make your own herb vinegars by steeping a small bunch of herbs, such as tarragon or thyme, in a bottle of white wine vinegar.

meat

beef stew

serves 4

ingredients

3 pounds boneless
chuck steak, cut into
2-inch pieces
2 tablespoons vegetable oil
2 onions, cut into
1-inch pieces

3 tablespoons
all-purpose flour
3 garlic cloves, finely
chopped
4 cups beef stock

3 carrots, cut into
1-inch lengths
2 celery stalks, cut into
1-inch lengths
1 tablespoon ketchup
1 bay leaf

¼ teaspoon dried thyme
¼ teaspoon dried rosemary
8 white round potatoes,
about 2 pounds, scrubbed
and cut into large chunks
salt and pepper

>1 Season the steak generously with salt and pepper. Heat the oil in a dutch oven or large, flameproof casserole dish over high heat.

>2 When the oil begins to smoke, add the steak and cook, stirring frequently, for 5–8 minutes, until well browned. Using a slotted spoon, transfer to a bowl.

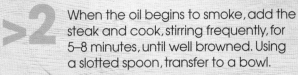

>3 Reduce the heat to medium, add the onions to the pot, and cook, stirring occasionally, for 5 minutes, until translucent.

>4 Stir in the flour and cook, stirring continuously, for 2 minutes. Add the garlic and cook for 1 minute.

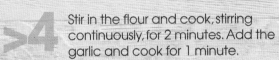

11

>**5** Beat in 1 cup of the stock and cook, scraping up all the sediment from the bottom of the pot.

>**6** Stir in the remaining stock and add the carrots, celery, ketchup, bay leaf, thyme, rosemary, and 1 teaspoon of salt. Return the steak to the pot.

>**7** Bring back to a gentle simmer, cover, and cook over low heat for 1 hour. Add the potatoes, replace the lid, and simmer for an additional 30 minutes.

>**8** Remove the lid, increase the heat to medium, and cook, stirring occasionally, for an additional 30 minutes, or until the meat and vegetables are tender. If the stew becomes too thick, add a little more stock or water.

Let stand for 15 minutes before serving.

meatballs with red peppers & tomato sauce

serves 4

ingredients

1 tablespoon olive oil
1 small onion, finely
  chopped
2 garlic cloves, finely
  chopped

2 fresh thyme sprigs, finely
  chopped
1½ pounds ground
  chuck beef
½ cup fresh bread crumbs
1 egg, lightly beaten
salt and pepper

sauce

1 onion, cut into wedges
3 red bell peppers, halved
  and seeded
1 (14½-ounce) can diced
  tomatoes
1 bay leaf

14

>1 Heat the oil in a skillet. Add the onion and garlic and cook over low heat for 5 minutes, until soft. Place in a bowl with the thyme, beef, bread crumbs, and egg.

>2 Season with salt and pepper, mix together thoroughly, and shape into 20 balls. Heat a large skillet over medium–low heat. Add the meatballs and cook, stirring gently, for 15 minutes, until lightly browned.

>3 Meanwhile, to make the sauce, preheat the broiler. Cook the onion wedges and red bell pepper halves under the preheated broiler, turning frequently, for 10 minutes, until the pepper skins are blistered and charred.

>4 Put the bell peppers into a plastic food bag, tie the top, and let cool. Set the onion wedges aside. Peel off the bell pepper skins, then coarsely chop the flesh.

15

>5 Put the bell pepper flesh into a food processor with the onion wedges and tomatoes. Process to a smooth puree and season with salt and pepper.

 >6 Pour into a saucepan with the bay leaf and bring to a boil. Reduce the heat and simmer, stirring occasionally, for 10 minutes. Remove and discard the bay leaf.

Serve the sauce immediately with the meatballs.

hamburgers with basil & chiles

serves 4

ingredients

1½ pounds ground
 chuck beef
1 red bell pepper, seeded
 and finely chopped
1 garlic clove, finely
 chopped
2 small red chiles, seeded
 and finely chopped
1 tablespoon chopped
 fresh basil
½ teaspoon ground cumin
salt and pepper
fresh basil sprigs, to garnish
hamburger buns, to serve

> **>1** Preheat the broiler to medium–high. Put the beef, red bell pepper, garlic, chiles, chopped basil, and cumin into a bowl.

> **>2** Mix together until well combined and season with salt and pepper.

Garnish with basil sprigs and serve immediately in hamburger buns.

> **3** Using your hands, form the mixture into four patty shapes. Place the burgers under the preheated broiler and cook for 5–8 minutes.

> **4** Turn and cook on the other side for 5–8 minutes, or until cooked through.

lasagna

serves 4

ingredients

2 tablespoons olive oil
2 ounces pancetta or bacon, chopped
1 onion, chopped
1 garlic clove, finely chopped

8 ounces ground sirloin beef
2 celery stalks, chopped
2 carrots, chopped
pinch of sugar
½ teaspoon dried oregano

1 (14½-ounce) can diced tomatoes
2 teaspoons Dijon mustard
2 cups store-bought cheese sauce

8 ounces oven-ready lasagna noodles
1½ cups freshly grated Parmesan cheese, plus extra for sprinkling
salt and pepper

>1 Preheat the oven to 375°F. Heat the oil in a large, heavy saucepan. Add the pancetta and cook over medium heat, stirring occasionally, for 3 minutes.

>2 Add the onion and garlic and cook, stirring occasionally, for 5 minutes, or until soft.

>3 Add the beef and cook, breaking it up with a wooden spoon, until brown all over. Stir in the celery and carrots and cook for 5 minutes.

>4 Season with salt and pepper. Add the sugar, oregano, and tomatoes and their can juices. Bring to a boil, reduce the heat, and simmer for 30 minutes.

>5 Meanwhile, stir the mustard into the cheese sauce.

 >6 In a large, rectangular ovenproof dish, make alternate layers of meat sauce, lasagna noodles, and Parmesan cheese.

 >7 Pour the cheese sauce over the layers, covering them completely, and sprinkle with Parmesan cheese.

>8 Bake in the preheated oven for 30 minutes, or until golden brown and bubbling.

Serve immediately.

paprika steak wraps with horseradish cream

serves 4

ingredients

4 tenderloin steaks, about
  6 ounces each
1 garlic clove, crushed
2 teaspoons smoked
  paprika, plus extra for
  sprinkling
sunflower oil, for brushing
½ cup crème fraîche
  or sour cream
3 tablespoons creamed
  horseradish
8 small flour tortillas
4 cups arugula leaves
2 firm, ripe avocados,
  peeled, pitted, and sliced
1 red onion, thinly sliced
salt and pepper

>1 Spread the steaks with the garlic and sprinkle both sides with the paprika. Season with salt and pepper.

>2 Preheat a ridged grill pan until hot and brush with oil. Add the steaks and cook for 6–8 minutes, turning once. Remove from the heat and let rest for 5 minutes.

Serve the wraps with a spoonful of horseradish cream, sprinkled with extra paprika.

>3 Mix together the crème fraîche and horseradish, then spread half over the tortillas.

>4 Slice the steaks into strips. Divide among the tortillas with the arugula, avocado, and red onion, wrapping the sides over.

grilled steak with hot chili salsa

serves 4

ingredients
sunflower oil, for brushing
4 tenderloin steaks, about
  8 ounces each
salt and pepper

hot chili salsa
4 fresh red habanero chiles
4 fresh green poblano chiles
3 tomatoes, peeled,
  seeded, and diced
2 tablespoons chopped
  fresh cilantro
1 tablespoon red wine
  vinegar
2 tablespoons olive oil
mache or other salad
  greens, to garnish

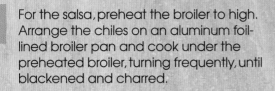

>1 For the salsa, preheat the broiler to high. Arrange the chiles on an aluminum foil-lined broiler pan and cook under the preheated broiler, turning frequently, until blackened and charred.

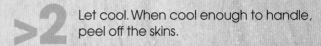

>2 Let cool. When cool enough to handle, peel off the skins.

>3 Halve and seed the chiles, then finely chop the flesh.

>4 Mix together the chiles, tomatoes, and cilantro in a bowl.

>5 Mix together the vinegar and olive oil in a small bowl or pitcher. Season with salt and pour it over the salsa. Toss well, cover, and chill until required.

>6 Heat a ridged grill pan over medium heat and brush lightly with sunflower oil. Season the steaks with salt and pepper, and cook for 2–4 minutes on each side, or until cooked to your liking.

Serve immediately with the salsa,
garnished with mache.

meatloaf

serves 6–8

ingredients

2 tablespoons butter
1 tablespoon olive oil, plus extra for brushing
3 garlic cloves, peeled
2 carrots, finely diced
1 celery stalk, finely diced
1 onion, finely diced

1 red bell pepper, seeded and finely diced
4 large white button mushrooms, finely diced
1 teaspoon dried thyme
2 teaspoons finely chopped rosemary

1 teaspoon Worcestershire sauce
⅓ cup ketchup
½ teaspoon cayenne pepper
2½ pounds ground sirloin beef, chilled

2 eggs, beaten
1 cup fresh bread crumbs
2 tablespoons packed brown sugar
1 tablespoon Dijon mustard
salt and pepper

>1 Melt the butter with the oil and garlic in a large skillet. Add the vegetables and cook over medium heat, stirring frequently, for 10 minutes, until most of the moisture has evaporated.

>2 Remove from the heat and stir in the herbs, Worcestershire sauce, ¼ cup of ketchup, and cayenne pepper. Let cool.

>3 Preheat the oven to 325°F. Brush a 9-inch loaf pan with oil.

>4 Put the beef into a large bowl and gently break it up with your fingers. Add the vegetable mixture and eggs, season with salt and pepper, and mix gently with your fingers. Add the bread crumbs and mix.

>5 Transfer the meatloaf mixture to the loaf pan. Smooth the surface with a spatula and bake in the preheated oven for 30 minutes.

>6 Meanwhile, make a glaze by beating together the sugar, the remaining 2 tablespoons of ketchup, mustard, and a pinch of salt.

>7 Remove the meatloaf from the oven and spread the glaze evenly over the top. Return to the oven and bake for an additional 35–45 minutes, or until the internal temperature reaches 160°F on a meat thermometer.

>8 Remove from the oven and let rest for at least 15 minutes.

Slice thickly to serve.

pot roast with potatoes & dill

serves 6

ingredients

4–5 white round potatoes,
  scrubbed and cut into
  large chunks
2½ tablespoons
  all-purpose flour
1 teaspoon salt

¼ teaspoon pepper
1 rolled brisket, about
  1½ pounds
2 tablespoons vegetable oil
2 tablespoons butter
1 onion, finely chopped

2 celery stalks, diced
2 carrots, peeled and diced
1 teaspoon dill seed
1 teaspoon dried thyme
  or oregano
1½ cups red wine

⅔–1 cup beef stock
2 tablespoons chopped
  fresh dill, to serve

> **1** Bring a large saucepan of lightly salted water to a boil. Add the potatoes, bring back to a boil, and cook for 10 minutes. Drain and set aside.

> **2** Preheat the oven to 275°F. Mix together 2 tablespoons of the flour with the salt and pepper in a large shallow dish. Dip the meat in the flour to coat.

> **3** Heat the oil in a flameproof dutch oven or casserole dish, add the meat, and brown. Transfer to a plate. Add half the butter to the pot, then add the onion, celery, carrots, dill seed, and thyme and cook for 5 minutes.

> **4** Return the meat and juices to the pot. Pour in the wine and enough stock to reach one-third of the way up the meat and bring to a boil.

>5 Cover and cook in the oven for 3 hours, turning the meat every 30 minutes. Add the potatoes and more stock, if necessary, after 2 hours.

>6 When ready, transfer the meat and vegetables to a warm serving dish. Strain the cooking liquid to remove any solids, then return the liquid to the pot.

>7 Mix the remaining butter and flour to a paste.

>8 Bring the cooking liquid to a boil. Whisk in small pieces of the flour and butter paste, whisking continuously until the sauce is smooth.

Pour the sauce over the meat and
vegetables. Sprinkle with fresh dill and serve.

tagliatelle with a rich meat sauce

serves 4

ingredients

¼ cup olive oil, plus extra
 for drizzling
3 ounces pancetta or
 bacon, diced
1 onion, chopped
1 garlic clove, finely
 chopped

1 carrot, chopped
1 celery stalk, chopped
8 ounces ground sirloin beef
4 ounces chicken livers,
 chopped
2 tablespoons
 tomato puree

½ cup dry white wine
1 cup beef stock
1 tablespoon chopped
 fresh oregano
1 bay leaf
1 pound dried
 tagliatelle

salt and pepper
grated Parmesan cheese,
 to serve

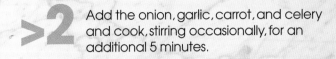

>1 Heat the oil in a large, heavy saucepan. Add the pancetta and cook over a medium heat, stirring occasionally, for 3–5 minutes, until it is just turning brown.

>2 Add the onion, garlic, carrot, and celery and cook, stirring occasionally, for an additional 5 minutes.

>3 Add the beef and cook over high heat, breaking up the meat with a wooden spoon, for 5 minutes, until browned.

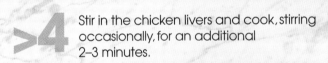

>4 Stir in the chicken livers and cook, stirring occasionally, for an additional 2–3 minutes.

> **5** Add the tomato puree, wine, stock, oregano, and bay leaf and season with salt and pepper. Bring to a boil, reduce the heat, cover, and simmer for 30–35 minutes.

> **6** Meanwhile, bring a large saucepan of lightly salted water to a boil. Add the pasta, bring back to a boil, and cook according to the package directions, until tender but still firm to the bite.

> **7** Drain the pasta and transfer to a warm serving dish. Drizzle with a little oil and toss well.

> **8** Remove and discard the bay leaf from the sauce, then pour the sauce over the pasta and toss again.

Serve immediately with grated Parmesan.

burritos

serves 4

ingredients

1 tablespoon olive oil
1 onion, chopped
1 garlic clove, finely
  chopped
1 pound ground sirloin beef
3 large tomatoes, seeded
  and chopped

1 red bell pepper, seeded
  and chopped
3 cups drained and rinsed
  canned mixed beans,
  such as red kidney beans,
  white kidney beans, and
  pinto beans

½ cup vegetable stock
1 tablespoon finely
  chopped fresh parsley
8 whole-wheat flour tortillas
½ cup tomato puree
½ cup shredded cheddar
  cheese

3 scallions, sliced
sea salt and pepper
mixed salad greens,
  to serve

42

> **1** Heat the oil in a large, nonstick skillet, add the onion and garlic, and cook until the onion is soft but not brown. Remove from the skillet.

> **2** Add the ground beef and cook over high heat, breaking it up with a wooden spoon, for 3–4 minutes, until beginning to brown. Drain off any excess oil.

> **3** Return the onion and garlic to the skillet, add the tomatoes and red pepper, and cook for 8–10 minutes.

> **4** Add the beans, stock, and parsley, season with salt and pepper, and cook, uncovered, for an additional 20–30 minutes, until well thickened.

>5 Meanwhile, preheat the oven to 350°F. Mash the meat mixture to break up the beans, then divide among the tortillas.

>6 Roll up each tortilla and place seam side down in a baking pan.

>7 Pour the tomato puree over the burritos and sprinkle with the cheese. Bake in the preheated oven for 20 minutes.

>8 Remove from the oven and spread the scallions over the burritos.

Transfer to a serving plate and serve with mixed salad greens.

beef chop suey

serves 4

ingredients

1 pound rib-eye steak, sliced
1 head broccoli, cut into florets
2 tablespoons vegetable oil
1 onion, sliced
2 celery stalks, sliced
1½ cups diagonally halved
   snow peas
½ cup of drained, canned
   bamboo shoots, rinsed
   and shredded
8 water chestnuts, sliced
3 cups sliced white button
   mushrooms
1 tablespoon oyster sauce
1 teaspoon salt

marinade

1 tablespoon Chinese rice wine
½ teaspoon white pepper
½ teaspoon salt
1 tablespoon light soy sauce
½ teaspoon sesame oil

> **1** Combine all the marinade ingredients in a bowl, and marinate the beef for at least 20 minutes.

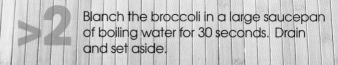

> **2** Blanch the broccoli in a large saucepan of boiling water for 30 seconds. Drain and set aside.

Transfer to bowls and serve immediately.

> **3** In a preheated wok, heat 1 tablespoon of the oil and stir-fry the beef until it begins to brown. Remove and set aside.

> **4** Clean the wok, heat the remaining oil, and sauté the onion for 1 minute. Add the celery and broccoli and cook for 2 minutes, Add the snow peas, bamboo shoots, water chestnuts, and mushrooms and cook for 1 minute. Add the beef and season with the oyster sauce and salt.

beef chow fun

serves 4

ingredients

12 ounces tenderloin
  or top sirloin beef
2 tablespoons soy sauce
2 tablespoons sesame oil

8 ounces flat rice noodles
2 tablespoons peanut oil
1 onion, sliced into thin
  wedges

2 garlic cloves, crushed
1-inch piece fresh ginger,
  chopped
1 red chile, thinly sliced

8 ounces baby broccoli cut
  into florets
½ head napa cabbage,
  sliced
chili oil, to serve

>1 Slice the beef into thin strips, place in a bowl, and sprinkle with soy sauce and sesame oil. Cover and let stand for 15 minutes.

>2 Prepare the noodles according to the package directions. Drain well. Transfer to a serving plate and keep warm.

>3 Heat 1 tablespoon of peanut oil in a wok and cook the beef over high heat until evenly browned. Remove and set aside.

>4 Add the remaining oil and sauté the onion, garlic, ginger, and chile for 1 minute.

>5 Add the broccoli and stir-fry for 2 minutes, then add the cabbage and stir-fry for 1 minute.

>6 Add the beef with any marinade juices and stir until thoroughly heated, then spoon the mixture onto the noodles.

Serve immediately, drizzled with chili oil.

sliced beef in black bean sauce

serves 4

ingredients

3 tablespoons peanut oil
1 pound tenderloin beef,
 thinly sliced
1 red bell pepper, seeded
 and thinly sliced
1 green bell pepper, seeded
 and thinly sliced
1 bunch scallions, sliced
2 garlic cloves, crushed
1 tablespoon grated fresh
 ginger
2 tablespoons black bean
 sauce
1 tablespoon sherry
1 tablespoon soy sauce

>1 Heat 2 tablespoons of the oil in a wok, add the sliced beef, and cook over high heat for 1–2 minutes, until browned. Remove and set aside.

>2 Add the remaining oil and bell peppers and stir-fry for 2 minutes.

Transfer to bowls and serve.

> **3** Add the scallions, garlic, and ginger and stir-fry for 30 seconds.

> **4** Add the black bean sauce, sherry, and soy sauce, then stir in the beef and heat until bubbling.

teriyaki steak

serves 4

ingredients

4 Porterhouse steaks, New York strip steaks, or skirt steaks, about 1 inch thick and 6 ounces each

2 tablespoons vegetable oil
2 cups fresh bean sprouts
4 scallions, trimmed and finely sliced
salt and pepper

teriyaki sauce

2 tablespoons mirin (Japanese rice wine)
2 tablespoons sake or pale dry sherry

¼ cup dark soy sauce
1 teaspoon granulated sugar

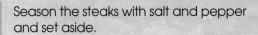

> **>1** Season the steaks with salt and pepper and set aside.

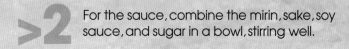

> **>2** For the sauce, combine the mirin, sake, soy sauce, and sugar in a bowl, stirring well.

> **>3** Heat 1 tablespoon of the oil in a skillet over high heat. Add the bean sprouts and cook quickly, tossing in the hot oil for 30 seconds.

> **>4** Remove from the skillet, drain on paper towels, and keep warm.

>5 Add the remaining oil to the skillet and, when hot, add the steaks. Cook for about 2–5 minutes on each side, or until cooked to your liking. Remove from the skillet and keep warm.

>6 Remove the skillet from the heat and add the sauce and scallions. Return to the heat and simmer for 2 minutes, stirring until the sauce thickens slightly and is glossy.

Slice each steak and arrange on a bed of
bean sprouts. Spoon the sauce over the steak
and serve immediately.

risotto with prosciutto

serves 4

ingredients
1 tablespoon olive oil
2 tablespoons butter
1 large onion, finely
  chopped
2 cups risotto rice
about 15 saffron threads
⅔ cup white wine
3½ cups simmering
  chicken stock
8 sun-dried tomatoes in
  olive oil, drained and
  cut into strips
⅔ cup frozen peas, thawed
2 ounces prosciutto,
  shredded
1 cup freshly grated
  Parmesan cheese, plus
  extra to serve
salt and pepper

> **1** Heat the oil and butter in a deep saucepan over medium heat until the butter has melted. Add the onion and cook for 5 minutes, until the onion is soft.

> **2** Reduce the heat, add the rice and saffron, and mix to coat. Cook, stirring continuously, for 2–3 minutes, until the grains are translucent. Add the wine and cook, stirring continuously, until reduced.

Spoon onto warm plates, sprinkle with Parmesan cheese, and serve immediately.

>3 Gradually add the hot stock, a ladleful at a time. Stir continuously, adding more liquid as the rice absorbs each addition. Cook for 10 minutes, then stir in the tomatoes.

>4 Cook for 8 minutes, then add the peas and ham. Stir and cook for 2–3 minutes, or until all the liquid is absorbed and the rice is creamy but still firm to the bite. Remove from the heat, season with salt and pepper, and stir in the cheese.

pork chops with applesauce

serves 4

ingredients
4 pork rib chops on the
 bone, each about
 1¼ inches thick,
 at room temperature
1½ tablespoons sunflower oil
salt and pepper

applesauce
3 cooking apples, such as
 Granny Smith, peeled,
 cored, and diced
¼ cup granulated sugar
finely grated zest of
 ½ lemon
½ tablespoon lemon juice
¼ cup water
¼ teaspoon ground
 cinnamon
pat of butter

> **>1** Preheat the oven to 400°F. To make the applesauce, put the first five ingredients into a heavy saucepan over high heat and bring to a boil, stirring.

> **>2** Reduce the heat to low, cover, and simmer for 15–20 minutes, until the apples are soft. Add the cinnamon and butter and beat until you have the desired consistency. Remove from the heat, cover, and keep warm.

Transfer the chops to warm plates and spoon the pan juices over them. Serve immediately, with the applesauce.

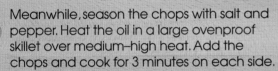**>3** Meanwhile, season the chops with salt and pepper. Heat the oil in a large ovenproof skillet over medium–high heat. Add the chops and cook for 3 minutes on each side.

>4 Transfer the skillet to the oven and roast the chops for 7–9 minutes, until the meat is opaque and the juices run clear when you cut through it, or a meat thermometer reads 145°F. Remove from the oven, cover with foil, and let stand for 3 minutes.

chorizo & chickpea casserole

serves 4

ingredients

2 tablespoons olive oil
1 onion, sliced
1 large yellow bell pepper, seeded and sliced
1 garlic clove, crushed

1 teaspoon crushed red pepper
8 ounces chorizo sausage
1 (14½-ounce) can diced tomatoes

1 (15-ounce) can chickpeas, drained and rinsed
1 cup long-grain rice
handful of arugula leaves

salt and pepper
¼ cup coarsely chopped fresh basil, to garnish

>1 Heat the oil in a dutch oven or flameproof casserole dish and sauté the onion over medium heat, stirring occasionally, for 5 minutes.

>2 Add the yellow bell pepper, garlic, and crushed red pepper and cook for 2 minutes, stirring.

>3 Chop the chorizo into bite-size chunks and stir into the pot.

>4 Add the tomatoes and chickpeas, and season with salt and pepper. Bring to a boil, cover, and simmer for 10 minutes.

>5 Meanwhile, cook the rice in a saucepan of lightly salted boiling water according to the package directions, until tender. Drain.

>6 Stir the arugula into the casserole.

Serve the casserole spooned over the rice,
garnished with fresh basil.

pork & rosemary burgers

serves 4

ingredients

1 pound fresh ground pork
1 small onion, finely
  chopped
1 garlic clove, crushed
1 tablespoon finely
  chopped fresh rosemary
oil, for brushing
1 small French baguette,
  split and cut into four
2 tomatoes, sliced
4 gherkin pickles, sliced
¼ cup Greek-style yogurt
2 tablespoons chopped
  fresh mint
salt and pepper

>**1** Put the pork, onion, garlic, and rosemary into a bowl, season with salt and pepper, and mix together with your hands.

>**2** Divide the mixture into four and shape into flat patty shapes.

Spoon the minty yogurt over the burgers and replace the baguette tops to serve.

> **>3** Brush a ridged grill pan or skillet with oil and cook the patties for 6–8 minutes, turning once, until golden and cooked through.

> **>4** Place a burger on the bottom half of each piece of baguette and top with the tomatoes and gherkins. Mix together the yogurt and mint.

pad thai noodles with pork strips & shrimp

serves 4

ingredients

8 ounces flat rice noodles
8 ounces pork tenderloin
3 tablespoons peanut oil
2 shallots, finely chopped
2 garlic cloves, finely chopped

6 ounces shrimp, peeled and deveined
2 eggs, beaten
2 tablespoons Thai fish sauce
juice of 1 lime

1 tablespoon ketchup
2 teaspoons packed light brown sugar
½ teaspoon crushed red pepper
1 cup bean sprouts

¼ cup roasted salted peanuts, chopped
6 scallions, diagonally sliced

>1 Prepare the noodles according to the package directions. Drain well.

>2 Slice the pork into strips about ¼ inch thick.

>3 Heat the oil in a wok and sauté the shallots for 1–2 minutes to soften.

>4 Add the pork strips and stir-fry for 2–3 minutes until cooked through.

>5 Add the garlic and shrimp and stir-fry for 1–2 minutes.

>6 Pour in the beaten eggs and stir for a few seconds until lightly set.

>7 Reduce the heat and add the noodles, fish sauce, lime juice, ketchup, and sugar. Toss together and heat through.

>8 Sprinkle with crushed red pepper, bean sprouts, peanuts, and scallions.

pork in plum sauce

serves 4

ingredients

1¼ pounds pork tenderloin
2 tablespoons peanut oil
1 orange bell pepper,
  seeded and sliced

1 bunch scallions, sliced
8 ounces oyster mushrooms,
  sliced
3 cups fresh bean sprouts

2 tablespoons dry sherry
⅔ cup plum sauce
8 ounces medium
  egg noodles

salt and pepper
chopped fresh cilantro,
  to garnish

>1 Slice the pork into long, thin strips.

>2 Heat the oil in a wok and stir-fry the pork for 2–3 minutes until cooked through.

>3 Add the orange bell pepper and stir-fry for 2 minutes, then add the scallions, mushrooms, and bean sprouts.

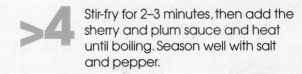

>4 Stir-fry for 2–3 minutes, then add the sherry and plum sauce and heat until boiling. Season well with salt and pepper.

>5 Meanwhile, cook the noodles in a saucepan of lightly salted boiling water according to the package directions, until tender.

>6 Drain the noodles, then add to the wok and toss well.

Serve immediately, garnished with fresh cilantro.

pork with beans

serves 4

ingredients

1¼ cups dried cranberry
  beans, soaked overnight
1¾ pounds pork shoulder
1 large onion, chopped
2 celery stalks, chopped
1 large carrot, chopped
1 fresh red chile, finely
  chopped
2 garlic cloves, finely
  chopped
large sprig of each fresh
  rosemary, thyme, and
  bay leaves
about 2½ cups chicken stock
salt and pepper
crusty bread, to serve

>1 Preheat the oven to 325°F. Drain and rinse the beans, put into a saucepan with fresh water, bring to a boil, and cook for 10 minutes. Drain and transfer to a wide dutch oven or casserole dish.

>2 Cut the pork into bite-size chunks, leaving on any skin.

Serve the pork and beans with chunks of bread to soak up the juices.

> **>3** Layer the pork and vegetables over the beans, sprinkling the layers with the chile and garlic and seasonsing with salt and pepper. Tuck in the herb sprigs.

> **>4** Pour in just enough stock to cover the meat, then cover and bake in the preheated oven, without stirring, for 3 hours, until tender.

honeyed apricot lamb with lemon couscous

serves 4

ingredients

4 lamb chops
4 teaspoons ground
  coriander
1 tablespoon ground cumin
1 small butternut squash

1 tablespoon olive oil
1 onion, chopped
2½ cups chicken stock
2 tablespoons chopped
  fresh ginger

¾ cup dried apricots
2 tablespoons honey
finely grated rind and juice
  of 1 lemon
1 cup couscous

salt and pepper
3 tablespoons chopped
  fresh mint, to garnish

> **1** Sprinkle the lamb chops with the ground coriander and cumin.

> **2** Peel and seed the squash and cut into bite-size chunks.

> **3** Heat the oil in a dutch oven or flameproof casserole dish. Add the lamb and cook over high heat for 2–3 minutes, turning once.

> **4** Stir in the squash, onion, and half the stock, then bring to a boil.

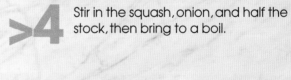

>5 Add the ginger, apricots, honey, and lemon juice and season with salt and pepper. Cover and cook over medium heat for about 20 minutes, stirring occasionally.

>6 Meanwhile, bring the remaining stock to a boil in a small saucepan, then stir in the couscous and lemon rind and season with salt and pepper. Remove from the heat, cover, and let stand for 5 minutes.

Serve the lamb with the couscous,
sprinkled with fresh mint.

orange & lemon crispy lamb chops

serves 2

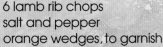

ingredients
1 garlic clove, crushed
1 tablespoon olive oil
2 tablespoons finely grated
  orange rind
2 tablespoons finely grated
  lemon rind
6 lamb rib chops
salt and pepper
orange wedges, to garnish

>**1** Preheat a ridged grill pan.

>**2** Mix together the garlic, oil, and citrus rinds in a bowl and season with salt and pepper.

Garnish with orange wedges
and serve.

>**3** Brush the mixture over the lamb chops.

>**4** Cook the cutlets in the preheated grill pan for 4–5 minutes on each side.

poultry

chicken noodle soup

serves 4–6

ingredients

2 skinless, boneless
  chicken breasts
9 cups water
1 onion, with skin left on,
  cut in half

1 large garlic clove,
  cut in half
½-inch piece fresh ginger,
  peeled and sliced
4 black peppercorns,
  lightly crushed

4 cloves
2 star anise
1 celery stalk, chopped
6 whole baby corn, sliced
2 scallions, finely shredded

4 ounces dried rice
  vermicelli noodles
1 carrot, peeled and
  shredded
salt and pepper

>1 Put the chicken breasts and water into a large saucepan and bring to a boil. Reduce the heat and simmer, skimming the surface until no more foam rises.

>2 Add the onion, garlic, ginger, peppercorns, cloves, star anise, and a pinch of salt.

>3 Continue to simmer for 20 minutes, or until the chicken is tender and there is no sign of pink when you cut through the center of the meat.

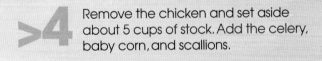

>4 Remove the chicken and set aside about 5 cups of stock. Add the celery, baby corn, and scallions.

> **5** Bring the stock to a boil and boil until the baby corn is almost tender, then add the noodles and continue boiling for 2 minutes.

> **6** Meanwhile, chop the chicken, add to the pan with the shredded carrot and continue cooking for about 1 minute, until the chicken is reheated and the noodles are soft. Season with salt and pepper.

Transfer to bowls and serve.

cream of chicken soup

serves 4

ingredients

3 tablespoons butter
4 shallots, chopped
1 leek, sliced
1 pound skinless, boneless
  chicken breasts, chopped

2½ cups chicken stock
1 tablespoon chopped
  fresh parsley
1 tablespoon chopped
  fresh thyme, plus extra
  sprigs to garnish

¾ cup heavy cream
salt and pepper

> **>1** Melt the butter in a large saucepan over medium heat. Add the shallots and cook, stirring, for 3 minutes, until slightly softened.

> **>2** Add the leek and cook for an additional 5 minutes, stirring.

> **>3** Add the chicken, stock, and herbs, and season with salt and pepper. Bring to a boil, reduce the heat, and simmer for 25 minutes, until the chicken is tender and cooked through.

> **>4** Remove from the heat and let cool for 10 minutes. Transfer the soup to a food processor or blender and process until smooth (you may need to do this in batches).

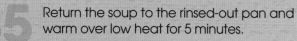

>5 Return the soup to the rinsed-out pan and warm over low heat for 5 minutes.

>6 Stir in the cream and cook for an additional 2 minutes, then remove from the heat and ladle into serving bowls.

Garnish with thyme sprigs and
serve immediately.

ginger & soy chicken wings

serves 4

ingredients

12 chicken wings
2 garlic cloves,
 crushed
1-inch piece fresh ginger
2 tablespoons dark
 soy sauce
2 tablespoons lime juice
1 tablespoon honey
1 teaspoon chili sauce
2 teaspoons sesame oil
lime wedges, to serve

>1 Tuck the pointed tip of each wing under the thicker end to make a neat triangle.

>2 Mix together the garlic, ginger, soy sauce, lime juice, honey, chili sauce, and oil.

Transfer to a serving dish and serve hot, with lime wedges.

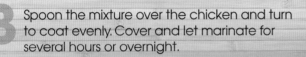 **>3** Spoon the mixture over the chicken and turn to coat evenly. Cover and let marinate for several hours or overnight.

>4 Preheat the broiler to hot. Cook the wings on an aluminum foil-lined broiler pan for 12–15 minutes, or until the chicken is tender and the juices run clear when a fork is inserted into the thickest part of the meat.

roasted chicken with lemon & thyme

serves 6

ingredients

5-pound chicken,
4 tablespoons butter,
softened
2 tablespoons chopped
fresh lemon thyme, plus
extra sprigs to garnish

1 lemon, cut into quarters
½ cup white wine, plus extra
if needed
salt and pepper

Preheat the oven to 425°F. Place the chicken in a roasting pan.

Put the butter in a bowl, then mix in the thyme, season with salt and pepper, and use to butter the chicken.

> 3 Place the lemon inside the cavity. Pour the wine over the chicken and roast in the preheated oven for 15 minutes.

> 4 Reduce the temperature to 375°F and roast, basting frequently, for an additional 1¾ hours.

>5 To check if the chicken is cooked through, pierce the thickest part of the thigh with a meat thermometer, which should read 165°F. Or pierce with the tip of a knife or a skewer; any juices should be clear with no traces of pink. Gently pull the leg away from the body; the leg should give. Transfer to a warm plate. Cover with aluminum foil and let rest for 10 minutes.

>6 Place the roasting pan on the stove and simmer the pan juices gently over low heat until they have reduced and are thick and glossy. Season with salt and pepper and reserve.

>7 To carve the chicken, place on a clean cutting board. Using a carving knife and fork, cut between the wings and the side of the breast. Remove the wings and cut slices off the breast.

>8 Cut the legs from the body and cut through the joint to make drumsticks and thigh portions.

Cut into slices and serve immediately
with the gravy.

chicken pot pies

makes 6

ingredients

1 tablespoon olive oil
3 cups sliced white button mushrooms,
1 onion, finely chopped
5 carrots, sliced
2 celery stalks, sliced

4 cups cold chicken stock
6 tablespoons butter
½ cup all-purpose flour, plus extra for dusting

2 pounds skinless, boneless chicken breasts, cut into 1-inch cubes
¾ cup frozen peas
1 teaspoon chopped fresh thyme

1½ sheets store-bought rolled dough pie crusts
1 egg, lightly beaten
salt and pepper

> **1** Preheat the oven to 400°F. Heat the oil in a large saucepan. Add the mushrooms and onion and cook over medium heat, stirring frequently, for 8 minutes, until golden.

> **2** Add the carrots, celery, and half the stock and bring to a boil. Reduce the heat to low and simmer for 12–15 minutes, until the vegetables are almost tender.

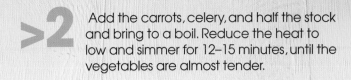

> **3** Meanwhile, melt the butter in a large saucepan over a medium heat. Whisk in the flour and cook, stirring constantly, for 4 minutes. Gradually whisk in the remaining stock, then reduce the heat to medium–low and simmer, stirring, until thick.

> **4** Stir into the vegetable mixture and add the chicken, peas and thyme.

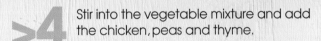

>5 Simmer, stirring continuously, for 5 minutes. Taste and adjust the seasoning, adding salt and pepper, if needed. Divide the mixture among six large ramekins (individual ceramic dishes).

>6 Roll out the dough on a floured surface and cut out 6 circles, each 1 inch larger than the diameter of the ramekins.

>7 Place the pie dough circles on top of the filling, then crimp the edges. Cut a small cross in the center of each circle.

>8 Put the ramekins on a baking sheet and brush the tops with beaten egg. Bake in the preheated oven for 35–40 minutes, until golden brown and bubbling.

Let stand for 15 minutes before serving.

chicken fajitas

serves 4

ingredients
3 tablespoons olive oil,
  plus extra for drizzling
3 tablespoons maple syrup
  or honey
1 tablespoon red wine
  vinegar
2 garlic cloves, crushed
2 teaspoons dried oregano
1–2 teaspoons crushed
  red pepper
4 skinless, boneless chicken
  breasts
2 red bell peppers, seeded
  and cut into 1-inch strips
salt and pepper
warm flour tortillas and
  shredded lettuce, to serve

> **1** Place the oil, maple syrup, vinegar, garlic, oregano, and crushed red pepper in a large, shallow dish, season with salt and pepper, and mix together.

> **2** Slice the chicken across the grain into 1-inch-thick slices. Toss in the marinade to coat. Cover and chill for 2–3 hours, turning occasionally.

Divide the chicken and bell peppers among the flour tortillas, top with a little shredded lettuce, wrap, and serve immediately.

>3 Drain the chicken, discarding the marinade. Heat a ridged grill pan until hot. Add the chicken and cook over medium–high heat for 3–4 minutes on each side until cooked through. Transfer to a warm plate and keep warm.

>4 Add the red peppers, skin side down, to the pan and cook for 2 minutes on each side until cooked through. Transfer to the plate with the chicken.

chicken wrapped in prosciutto with pesto

serves 4

ingredients

4 skinless, boneless chicken
 breasts
4 teaspoons green pesto
4 ounces mozzarella cheese

4 thin slices prosciutto
2 cups halved cherry
 tomatoes
⅓ cup dry white wine
 or chicken stock

1 tablespoon olive oil
salt and pepper
fresh ciabatta, to serve

> **1** Preheat the oven to 425°F. Place the chicken breasts on a board and cut a deep pocket into each with a sharp knife.

> **2** Place a teaspoonful of pesto in each pocket.

> **3** Cut the cheese into four equal pieces and divide among the chicken breasts, tucking into the pockets.

> **4** Wrap a slice of prosciutto around each chicken breast to enclose the filling, with the seam underneath.

>5 Place the chicken in a shallow ovenproof dish and arrange the tomatoes around it.

>6 Season with salt and pepper, pour the wine over the chicken, and drizzle with the oil.

>7 Bake in the preheated oven for 15–20 minutes, until the chicken is tender and the center is no longer pink when you cut into it.

>8 Cut the chicken breasts diagonally in half, place on serving plates with the tomatoes, and spoon the juices over them.

Serve the chicken with chunks of ciabatta
on the side.

chicken breasts with a parmesan crumb topping

serves 4

ingredients

4 skinless, boneless chicken
  breasts
⅓ cup pesto sauce
½ cup dried ciabatta bread
  crumbs

½ cup grated Parmesan
  cheese
finely grated rind of
  ½ lemon
2 tablespoons olive oil

salt and pepper
roasted vine tomatoes,
  to serve

>1 Preheat the oven to 425°F. Cut a deep slash into each chicken breast to make a pocket.

>2 Open out the chicken breasts and spread 1 tablespoon of the pesto into each pocket.

>3 Fold the chicken flesh back over the pesto and place in an ovenproof dish.

>4 Mix the remaining pesto with the bread crumbs, Parmesan cheese, and lemon rind.

> **5** Spread the bread-crumb mixture over the chicken breasts. Season with salt and pepper and drizzle with the oil.

> **6** Bake in the preheated oven for about 20 minutes, or until there is no sign of pink when the center of the meat is cut through.

Serve the chicken hot with roasted
vine tomatoes.

steamed chicken with chile & cilantro butter

serves 4

ingredients

4 tablespoons butter, softened

1 fresh Thai chile, seeded and chopped

3 tablespoons chopped fresh cilantro

4 skinless, boneless chicken breasts, about 6 ounces each

1¾ cups coconut milk

1½ cups chicken stock

1 cup long-grain rice

salt and pepper

pickled vegetables

1 carrot

½ cucumber

3 scallions

2 tablespoons rice vinegar

>1 Mix the butter with the chile and cilantro.

>2 Cut a deep slash into the side of each chicken breast to form a pocket.

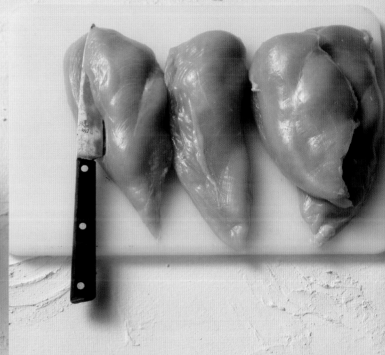

>3 Spoon one-quarter of the butter into each pocket and place on a 12-inch square of parchment paper.

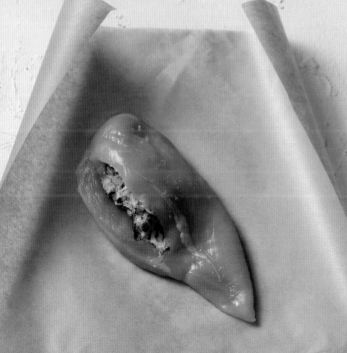

>4 Season with salt and pepper, then bring together two opposite sides of the paper on top, folding over to seal firmly. Twist the ends to seal.

>5 Pour the coconut milk and stock into a large saucepan with a steamer top. Bring to a boil. Stir in the rice with a pinch of salt.

>6 Place the chicken packages in the steamer top, cover, and simmer for 15–18 minutes, stirring the rice once, until the rice is tender and the chicken is no longer pink when you cut through the center of the meat.

>7 Meanwhile, trim the carrot, cucumber, and scallions and cut into fine matchsticks. Sprinkle with the rice vinegar.

>8 Unwrap the chicken, reserving the juices, and cut in half diagonally.

Serve the chicken over the rice, with the juices spooned over the meat and the pickled vegetables on the side.

chicken with creamy penne

serves 2

ingredients

8 ounces dried penne
1 tablespoon olive oil
2 skinless, boneless
  chicken breasts
4 tablespoons dry
  white wine
¾ cup frozen peas
⅓ cup heavy cream
salt
¼–⅓ cup chopped fresh
  parsley, to garnish

> **>1** Bring a large saucepan of lightly salted water to a boil. Add the pasta and cook according to the package directions, until tender but still firm to the bite.

> **>2** Meanwhile, heat the oil in a skillet, add the chicken, and cook over medium heat for about 4 minutes on each side.

Garnish with fresh parsley and serve.

>3 Pour in the wine and cook over high heat until it has almost evaporated and the chicken is tender and is no longer pink when you cut through the center of the meat.

>4 Drain the pasta. Add the peas, cream, and pasta to the skillet and stir well. Cover and simmer for 2 minutes.

chicken risotto with saffron

serves 4

ingredients

1 stick butter
2 pounds skinless, boneless
  chicken breasts,
  thinly sliced

1 large onion, chopped
2½ cups risotto rice
⅔ cup white wine
1 teaspoon crumbled
  saffron threads

5½ cups hot chicken stock
¾ cup grated Parmesan
  cheese
salt and pepper

> 1 Heat 4 tablespoons of the butter in a deep saucepan. Add the chicken and onion and cook, stirring frequently, for 8 minutes, or until golden brown and cooked through.

> 2 Add the rice and mix to coat in the butter. Cook, stirring continuously, for 2–3 minutes, or until the grains are translucent.

> 3 Add the wine and cook, stirring continuously, for 1 minute, until reduced.

> 4 Mix the saffron with ¼ cup of the hot stock. Add the liquid to the rice and cook, stirring continuously, until it is absorbed.

>5 Gradually add the remaining hot stock, a ladleful at a time. Add more liquid as the rice absorbs each addition. Cook, stirring, for 20 minutes, or until all the liquid is absorbed and the rice is creamy.

>6 Remove from the heat and add the remaining butter. Mix well, then stir in the Parmesan cheese until it melts. Season with salt and pepper.

Spoon the risotto into warm serving dishes
and serve immediately.

yakisoba

serves 2

ingredients

1 pound ramen noodles
1 onion, finely sliced
2 cups bean sprouts
1 red bell pepper, seeded
  and sliced
1 cup sliced, cooked
  chicken
12 cooked peeled
  shrimp
1 tablespoon oil,
  for stir-frying
2 tablespoons shoyu
½ tablespoon mirin
1 teaspoon sesame oil
1 teaspoon sesame seeds
2 scallions, finely sliced

> **>1** Cook the noodles according to the package directions, drain well, and transfer to a bowl.

> **>2** Mix together the onion, bean sprouts, red pepper, chicken, and shrimp in a bowl. Stir through the noodles. Meanwhile, preheat a wok over high heat, add the oil, and heat until very hot.

Sprinkle with sesame seeds and scallions and serve.

>3 Add the noodle mixture and stir-fry for 4 minutes, or until golden, then add the shoyu, mirin, and sesame oil and toss together.

>4 Divide the noodles between two bowls.

chicken with cashew nuts

serves 4–6

ingredients

1 pound skinless, boneless chicken meat, cut into bite-size pieces

3 tablespoons light soy sauce

1 teaspoon Chinese rice wine

pinch of sugar

½ teaspoon salt

3 dried Chinese mushrooms, soaked in warm water for 20 minutes

2 tablespoons vegetable oil or peanut oil

4 slices of fresh ginger

1 teaspoon finely chopped garlic

1 red bell pepper, seeded and cut into 1-inch squares

¾ cup cashew nuts, toasted

> **1** Marinate the chicken in 2 tablespoons of the light soy sauce, rice wine, sugar, and salt for at least 20 minutes.

> **2** Squeeze any excess water from the mushrooms and finely slice, discarding any tough stems. Reserve the soaking water.

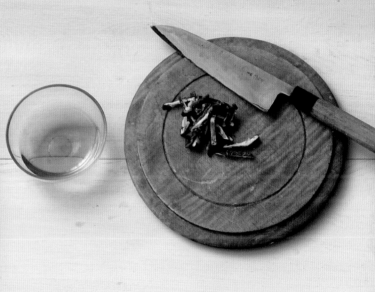

> **3** In a preheated wok, heat 1 tablespoon of the oil. Add the ginger and stir-fry until fragrant. Stir in the chicken and cook for 2 minutes, until it turns brown. Before the chicken is cooked through, remove and set aside.

> **4** Clean the wok, heat the remaining oil, and stir-fry the garlic until fragrant. Add the mushrooms and red pepper and stir-fry for 1 minute.

Add about 2 tablespoons of the mushroom soaking water and cook for about 2 minutes, until the water has evaporated.

>6 Return the chicken to the wok, add the remaining light soy sauce and the cashew nuts and stir-fry for 2 minutes, until the chicken is cooked through.

Transfer to bowls and serve.

green chicken curry
serves 4

ingredients
2 tablespoons peanut oil or
  vegetable oil
4 scallions, coarsely
  chopped
2 tablespoons green
  curry paste
3 cups canned
  coconut milk
1 chicken bouillon cube
6 skinless, boneless
  chicken breasts, cut
  into 1-inch cubes
large handful of fresh
  cilantro, chopped
1 teaspoon salt
cooked rice, to serve

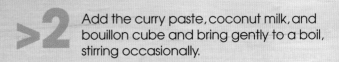

>1 Heat the oil in a preheated wok, add the scallions, and stir-fry over medium–high heat for 30 seconds, or until starting to soften.

>2 Add the curry paste, coconut milk, and bouillon cube and bring gently to a boil, stirring occasionally.

Serve immediately with rice.

>3 Add the chicken, half the cilantro, and the salt and stir well, making sure all the chicken is submerged in the liquid. Reduce the heat and simmer for 8–10 minutes, until the chicken is cooked through and tender.

>4 Stir in the remaining cilantro.

teriyaki chicken

serves 4

ingredients

4 boneless chicken breasts,
  about 6 ounces each,
  with or without skin
¼ cup prepared teriyaki
  sauce
peanut oil or corn oil,
  for brushing

sesame noodles

8 ounces dried thin
  buckwheat noodles
1 tablespoon toasted
  sesame oil
2 tablespoons sesame
  seeds, toasted

2 tablespoons finely
  chopped fresh parsley
salt and pepper

>1 Using a sharp knife, score each chicken breast diagonally across 3 times. Rub all over with teriyaki sauce. Set aside in the refrigerator to marinate for at least 10 minutes and up to 24 hours.

>2 Meanwhile, preheat the broiler to high. Bring a saucepan of water to a boil, add the buckwheat noodles, and cook according to the package directions. Drain and rinse well in cold water.

>3 Lightly brush a ridged grill pan with peanut oil. Add the chicken breasts, skin side up, and brush again with a little extra teriyaki sauce.

>4 Grill the chicken breasts, brushing them occasionally with extra teriyaki sauce, for 15 minutes, or until tender and the center is pink when you cut through the meat.

133

>5 Meanwhile, heat a wok over high heat. Add the sesame oil and heat until it shimmers.

>6 Add the noodles and stir around to heat through, then stir in the sesame seeds and parsley. Season with salt and pepper.

Transfer the chicken breasts to plates and
serve with the noodles

creamy turkey & broccoli gnocchi

serves 4

ingredients

1 tablespoon sunflower oil
1 pound turkey stir-fry strips
2 small leeks, sliced
 diagonally
1 pound store-bought fresh
 gnocchi
3 cups broccoli florets
½ cup crème fraîche
1 tablespoon whole-grain
 mustard
3 tablespoons orange juice
salt and pepper
¼ cup toasted pine nuts,
 to serve

> **>1** Heat the oil in a wok or large skillet, then add the turkey and leeks and stir-fry over high heat for 5–6 minutes until the turkey is cooked through.

> **>2** Meanwhile, bring a saucepan of lightly salted water to a boil. Add the gnocchi and broccoli, and cook for 3–4 minutes.

Serve immediately, sprinkled with pine nuts.

 3 Drain the gnocchi and broccoli and stir into the turkey mixture.

 4 Mix together the crème fraîche, mustard, and orange juice in a small bowl. Season with salt and pepper, then stir into the wok.

grilled turkey cutlets with lemon

serves 4

ingredients

1 lemon
2 tablespoons olive oil
1 garlic clove, crushed

4 turkey cutlets
salt and pepper
salad, to serve

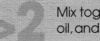

>1 Finely grate the rind from the lemon and squeeze the juice.

>2 Mix together the lemon rind, lemon juice, oil, and garlic in a wide, nonmetallic dish.

>3 Place the turkey cutlets in the lemon mixture, turning to coat evenly. Cover with plastic wrap and chill in the refrigerator for 30 minutes. Drain the turkey, discarding the marinade.

>4 Preheat a ridged grill pan to hot. Season the turkey with salt and pepper, place in the pan, and cook for about 4 minutes, until golden.

>5 Using tongs, turn the turkey cutlets over and cook the other side for 3–4 minutes, until the turkey is tender and the center is no longer pink when you cut through the meat.

>6 Transfer the turkey to a warm plate, cover with aluminum foil, and let stand for 3–4 minutes before serving.

Serve with salad.

turkey schnitzel with potato wedges

serves 4

ingredients

4 potatoes
2 tablespoons olive oil, plus
   extra for pan frying

1 tablespoon dried sage
1 cup fresh white bread
   crumbs

½ cup finely grated fresh
   Parmesan cheese
4 thinly sliced turkey cutlets

1 egg, beaten
salt and pepper
lemon wedges, to serve

>1 Preheat the oven to 425°F. Cut each potato into 8 wedges.

>2 Place the potato wedges in a bowl and add the oil and 1 teaspoon of the sage, then season with salt and pepper. Toss well to coat evenly.

>3 Arrange the potatoes in a single layer in a baking pan. Bake in the oven for about 25 minutes, until golden brown and tender.

>4 Meanwhile, mix together the bread crumbs, cheese, and remaining sage, and season with salt and pepper.

>5 Dip the turkey in the beaten egg and then in the crumb mixture, pressing to coat on both sides.

>6 Heat a shallow depth of oil in a skillet over fairly high heat, add the turkey, and cook for 4–5 minutes, turning once, until golden brown and the turkey is cooked through—there should be no signs of pink when cut through the center.

Serve the turkey hot with the potato and
lemon wedges.

turkey, broccoli & bok choy

serves 4

ingredients

1 pound turkey cutlets,
   skinned and cut into strips
1 cup long-grain rice
1 tablespoon vegetable oil
1 bunch broccoli,
   cut into florets

2 heads bok choy, washed
   and separated
1 red bell pepper, thinly
   sliced
¼ cup chicken stock
salt

marinade

1 tablespoon soy sauce
1 tablespoon honey
2 garlic cloves, crushed

>**1** To make the marinade, combine the ingredients in a medium bowl. Add the turkey and toss to coat. Cover with plastic wrap and marinate in the refrigerator for 2 hours.

>**2** Cook the rice in a saucepan of lightly salted water according to the package directions, until tender. Drain and keep warm.

>**3** Meanwhile, preheat a wok over medium–high heat, add the oil, and heat for 1 minute. Add the turkey and stir-fry for 3 minutes, or until the turkey is cooked through.

>**4** Remove the turkey with a slotted spoon, set aside, and keep warm. Add the broccoli, bok choy, and red pepper to the wok and stir-fry for 2 minutes.

>5 Add the stock and continue to stir-fry for 2 minutes, or until the vegetables are tender but still firm to the bite.

>6 Return the turkey to the wok and cook briefly to reheat.

hoisin & sesame-glazed broiled duck

serves 4

ingredients

2 duck breasts, about
 8 ounces each
½ teaspoon ground
 star anise
3 tablespoons hoisin sauce
1 tablespoon sesame oil
1 ripe mango
½ cucumber
4 scallions
1 tablespoon rice vinegar
toasted sesame seeds,
 to sprinkle

>1 Using a sharp knife, score the skin of the duck breast in a diamond pattern.

>2 Mix together the star anise, hoisin sauce, and sesame oil and brush over the duck. Cover and marinate for at least 30 minutes.

Serve the duck slices arranged over a spoonful of the mango salad, sprinkled with sesame seeds.

>3 Meanwhile, preheat the broiler to hot. Peel, pit, and thinly slice the mango. Cut the cucumber into matchsticks and thinly slice the onions. Stir together and sprinkle with vinegar.

>4 Broil the duck for 8–10 minutes on each side, brushing with the marinade. Rest for 5 minutes, then slice thinly.

151

duck breasts with citrus glaze

serves 4

ingredients

¼ cup firmly packed light
  brown sugar, plus extra
  if needed
finely grated rind and juice
  of 1 orange

finely grated rind and juice
  of 1 large lemon
finely grated rind and juice
  of 1 lime
4 duck breasts, skin on

2 tablespoons olive oil
salt and pepper
freshly cooked sugar snap
  peas and orange wedges,
  to serve

>1 Put the sugar in a small saucepan, add just enough water to cover, and heat gently until dissolved.

>2 Add the citrus rinds and juices and bring to a boil.

>3 Reduce the heat and simmer for about 10 minutes, until syrupy. Remove from the heat. Taste and add extra sugar, if needed. Keep warm.

>4 Meanwhile, score the skin of the duck breasts with a sharp knife in a diamond pattern and rub with salt and pepper.

>5 Heat the oil in a skillet. Place the duck breasts skin-side down in the skillet and cook for 5 minutes on each side, until the flesh is just pink.

>6 Slice the duck breasts diagonally into 5–6 slices and transfer to warm plates.

Arrange some sugar snap peas and orange wedges on each plate, spoon over the glaze, and serve immediately.

fish & seafood

broiled fish with lemon

serves 4

ingredients

olive oil, for brushing
4 white fish fillets, such as
  flounder, red snapper,
  or pollack, about
  6 ouces each

salt and pepper
lemon wedges, to serve

>1 Preheat the broiler to very hot. Brush the broiler pan or a shallow flameproof dish with oil.

>2 To remove the skin, place the fish skin side down and slide a sharp knife between the skin and the flesh, keeping the knife flat.

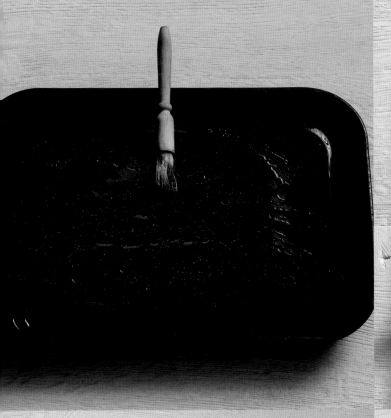

>3 Lay the fish in the prepared pan and brush with oil. Season with salt and pepper.

>4 Place under the broiler and cook for 3–4 minutes, until the surface of the fish is firm and white.

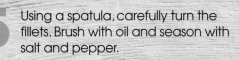

>5 Using a spatula, carefully turn the fillets. Brush with oil and season with salt and pepper.

>6 Broil the other side for 3–4 minutes, depending on the thickness, until the fish is firm and flakes easily with a fork.

Serve immediately with lemon wedges.

fish nuggets with chili mayonnaise

serves 4

ingredients

1½ cups all-purpose flour
3 eggs
1 cup matzo meal
1 pound firm white fish fillets,
  such as cod, red snapper,
  or pollack, cut into strips

sunflower oil or peanut oil,
  for pan frying
salt and pepper

chili mayonnaise

2 tablespoons sweet
  chili sauce
¼–⅓ cup mayonnaise

>1 Mix the flour with plenty of salt and pepper on a large flat plate.

>2 Beat the eggs in a bowl.

>3 Spread out the matzo meal on another flat plate.

>4 Dip the fish pieces into the seasoned flour, then into the beaten egg, then into the matzo meal, making sure there is a generous coating.

>5 Pour the oil into a nonstick skillet to a depth of ½ inch and heat. Cook the fish pieces, in batches, for a few minutes, turning once, until golden and cooked through. Keep the fish nuggets warm while you cook the remainder.

>6 To make the chili mayonnaise, put the chili sauce and mayonnaise in a bowl and beat together until combined.

Transfer the fish to warm plates and serve with the chili mayonnaise on the side.

peppered tuna steaks
serves 4

ingredients
4 tuna steaks, about
  6 ounces each
4 teaspoons sunflower oil
  or olive oil
1 teaspoon salt
2 tablespoons pink, green,
  and black peppercorns,
  coarsely crushed
handful of fresh arugula
  leaves, to garnish
lemon wedges, to serve

>1 Brush the tuna steaks with the oil.

>2 Sprinkle with the salt.

Garnish with arugula and serve with lemon wedges for squeezing over the fish.

> >3 Coat the fish in the crushed peppercorns.

> >4 Heat a ridged grill pan over medium heat. Add the tuna and cook for 2–3 minutes on each side.

tuna pasta casserole

serves 4

ingredients

8 ounces dried elbow
  macaroni
2 (5-ounce) cans chunk
  light tuna in oil, drained
  and flaked
1 small red onion, grated
2 tablespoons chopped
  fresh parsley
2 cups shredded American
  or cheddar cheese
1 extra-large egg, beaten
1 cup light cream
¼ teaspoon grated nutmeg
salt and pepper

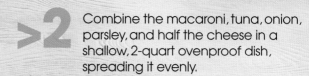

>1 Preheat the oven to 425°F and place a baking sheet on the middle shelf to heat. Bring a saucepan of lightly salted water to a boil, add the macaroni, and cook according to the package directions, or until tender but still firm to the bite. Drain.

>2 Combine the macaroni, tuna, onion, parsley, and half the cheese in a shallow, 2-quart ovenproof dish, spreading it evenly.

Serve hot.

> **>3** Beat the egg with the cream and nutmeg, and season with salt and pepper. Pour the sauce over the macaroni mixture and sprinkle with the remaining cheese.

> **>4** Place the dish on the preheated baking sheet in the oven and bake for about 15 minutes, until golden brown and bubbling.

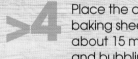

fish cakes

makes 8

ingredients

3 russet or Yukon gold
  potatoes, peeled
12 ounces cooked salmon,
  flaked
½ cup chopped fresh dill,
  plus extra to garnish
6 scallions, some green parts
  included, finely chopped

1 tablespoon coarsely
  grated lemon zest
1 tablespoon cornstarch,
  sifted
1 teaspoon salt
½ teaspoon pepper
2 eggs, lightly beaten
flour, for dusting
oil, for frying

garlic mayonnaise

3 large garlic cloves, peeled
1 teaspoon sea salt flakes
2 egg yolks, at room
  temperature
1 cup extra virgin olive oil
2 tablespoons lemon juice

> 1   Bring a large saucepan of water to a boil, add the potatoes, bring back to a boil, and cook for 20 minutes, or until tender. Drain well, mash, and set aside.

> 2   Put the salmon, potato, dill, scallions, and lemon zest into a large bowl and lightly mix with a fork.

> 3   Sprinkle with the cornstarch and season with salt and pepper. Stir in the beaten eggs.

> 4   With floured hands, form the mixture into 8 patties about ¾ inch thick.

> **5** Place on a baking sheet lined with wax paper and chill for at least 2 hours.

> **6** To make the garlic mayonnaise, use a mortar and pestle to crush the garlic and salt to a smooth paste. Transfer to a large bowl. Beat in the egg yolks.

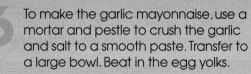

> **7** Add the oil, a few drops at a time, beating continuously, until thick and smooth. Beat in the lemon juice. Cover with plastic wrap and set aside.

> **8** Heat the oil in a skillet and cook the cakes over medium–high heat for 8 minutes, until golden. Turn and cook the other side for 4–5 minutes, until golden.

Garnish with dill and serve immediately with
the garlic mayonnaise.

steamed salmon

serves 4

ingredients

3 tablespoons butter,
 melted
4 salmon fillets, about
 5 ounces each
finely grated rind and juice
 of 1 lemon
1 tablespoon snipped
 chives
1 tablespoon chopped
 parsley
salt and pepper
salad and crusty bread,
 to serve

>1 Preheat the oven to 400°F. Cut four 12-inch squares of double thickness aluminum foil and brush with the melted butter.

>2 Place a piece of salmon on each square and spoon over the lemon rind and juice. Sprinkle with the chives and parsley and season with salt and pepper.

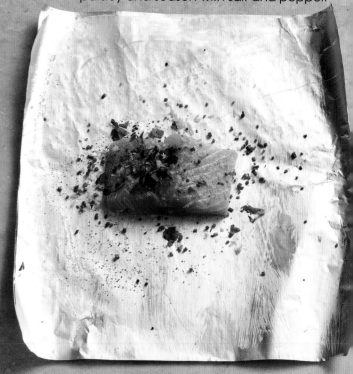

Transfer the salmon and juices to warm serving plates and serve immediately with salad and crusty bread.

> 3 Wrap the foil over loosely and seal firmly with the seam on top.

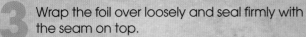

> 4 Place the packages on a baking sheet and bake for 20 minutes, or until the fish flakes easily.

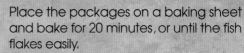

seared sesame salmon with bok choy

serves 4

ingredients

1-inch piece fresh ginger
1 tablespoon soy sauce
1 teaspoon sesame oil

4 skinless salmon fillets
2 tablespoons sesame
 seeds
lime wedges, to serve

stir-fry

2 small heads bok choy
1 bunch scallions
1 tablespoon sunflower oil

1 teaspoon sesame oil
salt and pepper

>1 Peel and finely grate the ginger and mix with the soy sauce and sesame oil in a shallow dish.

>2 Add the salmon fillets, turning to coat evenly on both sides.

>3 Sprinkle the salmon on one side with half the sesame seeds, then turn and sprinkle the other side with the remaining sesame seeds.

>4 Cut the bok choy lengthwise into quarters.

>5 Cut the scallions into thick diagonal slices.

>6 Preheat a heavy skillet. Add the salmon and cook for 3–4 minutes. Turn and cook for an additional 3–4 minutes.

>7 Meanwhile, heat the sunflower oil and sesame oil in a wok, add the bok choy and scallions, and stir-fry for 2–3 minutes. Season with salt and pepper.

>8 Divide the vegetables among warm serving plates and place a salmon fillet on top of each bed of vegetables.

Serve immediately with lime wedges for squeezing over the fish.

sea bass with olive gremolata

serves 4

ingredients

2 pounds small
  new potatoes
4 sea bass fillets, about
  6 ounces each

1 tablespoon olive oil
¼ cup dry white wine
salt and pepper

olive gremolata

grated rind of 1 lemon
1 garlic clove, chopped
2 large handfuls flat-leaf
  parsley (about 2 ounces)

¾ cup pitted ripe
  black olives
2 tablespoons capers
2 tablespoons olive oil

>1 Cook the potatoes in a saucepan of lightly salted boiling water for 15–20 minutes, or until tender.

>2 Meanwhile, make the gremolata. Place the lemon rind, garlic, parsley, olives, capers, and oil in a food processor and process briefly to form a coarse paste.

>3 Brush the sea bass with the oil and season with salt and pepper. Heat a heavy skillet and cook the sea bass for 5–6 minutes, turning once.

>4 Remove the fish from the skillet and keep warm. Stir the wine into the skillet and boil for 1 minute, stirring.

>5 Add the gremolata to the skillet and stir for a few seconds to heat gently.

 >6 Drain the potatoes when tender and crush lightly with a wooden spoon or vegetable masher.

Serve the sea bass and crushed potatoes topped with the gremolata.

monkfish kabobs with basil mayonnaise

serves 2–4

ingredients

1 garlic clove, crushed
finely grated rind and juice
  of 1 lemon
2 tablespoons olive oil

1 pound monkfish fillet,
  cut into 1¼-inch chunks
2 red onions, cut into thin
  wedges
salt and pepper

basil mayonnaise

2 egg yolks
1 tablespoon lemon juice
1 teaspoon Dijon mustard
⅔ cup sunflower oil

⅔ cup extra virgin olive oil
1¼ cups chopped fresh
  basil leaves

> **1** Mix together the garlic, lemon rind, lemon juice, and olive oil and season with salt and pepper. Stir in the fish, cover, and let marinate in the refrigerator for 30 minutes. If using wooden skewers, put them in a bowl of water to soak.

> **2** For the basil mayonnaise, beat together the egg yolks, lemon juice, and mustard until smooth.

> **3** Add the sunflower oil and beat until the mixture thickens.

> **4** Beat in the extra virgin olive oil in a thin, steady stream to make a thick, creamy sauce. Stir in the basil and adjust the seasoning, adding salt and pepper, if needed.

>5 Preheat the broiler to high. Drain the monkfish, reserving the marinade. Thread the monkfish and onion alternately onto 4 metal or presoaked wooden skewers.

>6 Cook the kabobs under the preheated broiler, turning occasionally and basting with the reserved marinade, for 6–8 minutes, until golden.

Serve the kabobs hot with the basil mayonnaise.

187

monkfish with a lemon & parsley crust

serves 4

ingredients
¼ cup sunflower oil
¼ cup fresh bread crumbs
¼ cup chopped fresh
  parsley, plus extra sprigs
  to garnish
finely grated rind of 1 large
  lemon
4 monkfish fillets, about
  5–6 ounces each
salt and pepper

> **1** Preheat the oven to 350°F. Mix together the oil, bread crumbs, parsley, and lemon rind in a bowl until well combined. Season with salt and pepper.

> **2** Place the fish fillets in a large roasting pan.

Garnish with parsley sprigs and serve.

>3 Divide the bread-crumb mixture among the fish and press it down with your fingers to make sure it covers the fillets.

>4 Bake in the preheated oven for 7–8 minutes, or until the fish is cooked through.

rustic fish stew

serves 4

ingredients

12 ounces fresh clams, scrubbed
2 tablespoons olive oil
1 large onion, chopped

2 garlic cloves, crushed
2 celery stalks, sliced
12 ounces firm white fish fillets, such as cod, red snapper, or pollack

8 ounces prepared squid rings
1¾ cups fish stock
6 plum tomatoes, chopped

small bunch of fresh thyme
salt and pepper
crusty bread, to serve

>1 Clean the clams under cold running water, scrubbing the shells. Discard any with broken shells and any that refuse to close when tapped.

>2 Heat the oil in a large saucepan and sauté the onion, garlic, and celery for 3–4 minutes, until softened but not browned.

>3 Meanwhile, cut the fish into chunks.

>4 Stir the fish and squid into the pan, then cook gently for 2 minutes.

>5 Stir in the stock, tomatoes, and thyme and season with salt and pepper. Cover and simmer gently for 3–4 minutes.

>6 Add the clams, cover, and cook over high heat for an additional 2 minutes, or until the shells open. Discard any that remain closed.

Serve the casserole immediately with chunks of bread.

paella

serves 6–8

ingredients

⅓ cup olive oil
6–8 boned chicken thighs
4 ounces Spanish chorizo
  sausage, sliced
2 large onions, chopped
4 large garlic cloves,
  crushed

1 teaspoon mild or hot
  Spanish paprika
2 cups paella rice or risotto
  rice, rinsed and drained
1 cup chopped green
  beans
1 cup frozen peas

5½ cups fish stock
½ teaspoon saffron threads,
  soaked in 2 tablespoons
  hot water
16 mussels, soaked in salted
  water for 10 minutes
16 shrimp, peeled and
  deveined

2 red bell peppers, halved
  and seeded, then broiled,
  peeled, and sliced
salt and pepper
freshly chopped parsley,
  to garnish

> **1** Heat 3 tablespoons of the oil in a 12-inch paella pan or flameproof casserole dish. Cook the chicken over medium–high heat, turning frequently, for 5 minutes, or until golden and crisp.

> **2** Using a slotted spoon, transfer to a bowl.

> **3** Add the chorizo to the pan and cook, stirring, for 1 minute, or until beginning to crisp, then add to the chicken.

> **4** Heat the remaining oil in the pan, add the onions, and cook, stirring, for 2 minutes.

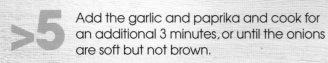

>5 Add the garlic and paprika and cook for an additional 3 minutes, or until the onions are soft but not brown.

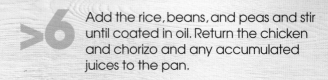

>6 Add the rice, beans, and peas and stir until coated in oil. Return the chicken and chorizo and any accumulated juices to the pan.

>7 Stir in the stock, saffron, and its soaking liquid, season with salt and pepper, and bring to a boil, stirring. Reduce the heat to low and simmer, uncovered, for 15 minutes.

>8 Discard any mussels with broken shells and any that refuse to close when tapped. Arrange the mussels, shrimp, and bell peppers on top. Cover and simmer for 5 minutes, until the shrimp turn pink, and the mussels open. Discard any mussels that remain closed. Ensure the chicken is cooked through.

Garnish with the parsley and
serve immediately.

thai shrimp noodle bowl

serves 4

ingredients

1 bunch scallions
2 celery stalks
1 red bell pepper
8 ounces rice vermicelli
   noodles

2 tablespoons peanut oil
⅓ cup unsalted peanuts
1 fresh Thai chile, sliced
1 lemongrass stalk, crushed

1¾ cups fish stock or
   chicken stock
1 cup coconut milk
2 teaspoons Thai fish sauce

12 ounces cooked, peeled
   jumbo shrimp
salt and pepper
¼ cup chopped fresh
   cilantro, to garnish

>1 Trim the scallions and celery and thinly slice diagonally. Seed and thinly slice the bell pepper.

>2 Prepare the noodles according to the package directions. Drain.

>3 Heat the oil in a wok and stir-fry the peanuts for 1–2 minutes, until golden. Lift out with a slotted spoon.

>4 Add the sliced scallions, celery, and red bell pepper to the wok and stir-fry over high heat for 1–2 minutes.

> **5** Add the chile, lemongrass, stock, coconut milk, and fish sauce and bring to a boil.

> **6** Stir in the shrimp and bring back to a boil, stirring. Season with salt and pepper, then add the noodles.

Transfer to warm bowls, garnish with cilantro, and serve.

ginger shrimp
with oyster mushrooms

serves 4

ingredients

⅔ cup chicken stock
2 teaspoons sesame seeds
1 tablespoon grated
 fresh ginger
1 tablespoon soy sauce

¼ teaspoon hot pepper
 sauce
1 teaspoon cornstarch
3 tablespoons vegetable oil
3 carrots, thinly sliced

12 ounces oyster
 mushrooms, thinly sliced
1 large red bell pepper,
 seeded and thinly sliced

1 pound jumbo shrimp,
 peeled and deveined
2 garlic cloves, crushed
fresh cilantro sprigs,
 to garnish
freshly cooked rice, to serve

> **1** In a small bowl, stir together the stock, sesame seeds, ginger, soy sauce, hot pepper sauce, and cornstarch until well blended. Set aside.

> **2** Add 2 tablespoons of the oil to a large wok and heat. Stir-fry the carrots for 3 minutes, remove from the wok, and set aside.

> **3** Add the remaining oil to the wok and stir-fry the mushrooms for 2 minutes. Remove from the wok and set aside.

> **4** Add the red bell pepper, shrimp, and garlic to the wok and stir-fry for 3 minutes, until the shrimp turn pink and start to curl.

203

>5 Stir the sauce again and pour it into the wok.

>6 Cook until the mixture bubbles, then return the carrots and mushrooms to the wok. Cover and cook for an additional 2 minutes, until heated through.

Garnish with cilantro sprigs and serve over
cooked rice.

wine-steamed mussels

serves 4

ingredients
1 stick butter
1 shallot, chopped
3 garlic cloves, finely
  chopped
4½ pounds fresh mussels,
  scrubbed and debearded
1 cup dry white wine
¼ cup chopped
  fresh parsley
salt and pepper
fresh crusty bread,
  to serve

>1 Place half the butter in a large saucepan and melt over low heat. Add the shallot and garlic and cook for 2 minutes.

>2 Discard any mussels with broken shells and any that refuse to close when tapped. Add the mussels and wine to the pan and season with salt and pepper. Cover and bring to a boil, then cook for 3 minutes, shaking the pan from time to time.

Serve immediately with fresh crusty bread for
mopping up the juices.

>3 Remove the mussels from the pan with
a slotted spoon and place in individual
serving bowls. Discard any mussels that
remain closed.

>4 Stir the remaining butter and the parsley
into the cooking juices in the pan. Bring
to a boil, then pour over the mussels.

seafood risotto

serves 4

ingredients

⅔ cup dry white wine

4 baby squid, cleaned and sliced

8 ounces shrimp, peeled and deveined

8 ounces fresh mussels, scrubbed and debearded

2 tablespoons olive oil

4 tablespoons butter

1 onion, finely chopped

2 garlic cloves, finely chopped

2 bay leaves

2 cups risotto rice

about 6 cups hot fish stock

salt and pepper

chopped fresh flat-leaf parsley, to garnish

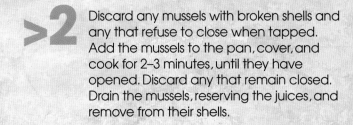

>1 Heat the wine in a saucepan until boiling. Add the squid and shrimp, cover, and cook for 2 minutes. Remove the squid and shrimp with a slotted spoon and set aside.

>2 Discard any mussels with broken shells and any that refuse to close when tapped. Add the mussels to the pan, cover, and cook for 2–3 minutes, until they have opened. Discard any that remain closed. Drain the mussels, reserving the juices, and remove from their shells.

>3 Heat the oil and butter in a deep saucepan. Add the onion and cook, stirring frequently, for 3–4 minutes, until softened.

>4 Add the garlic, bay leaves, and rice, and mix to coat in the butter and oil. Cook, stirring continuously, for 2–3 minutes, until the grains are translucent.

>5 Stir in the cooking juices from the mussels, then gradually add the hot stock, a ladleful at a time. Cook, stirring, for 15 minutes, until the liquid is absorbed and the rice is creamy.

>6 Stir in the cooked seafood, cover, and cook for an additional 2 minutes to heat through. Season with salt and pepper.

Serve the risotto immediately, sprinkled with parsley.

ravioli with crabmeat & ricotta

serves 4

ingredients

2⅓ cups type 00 pasta flour
  or all-purpose flour
1 teaspoon salt
3 eggs, beaten
5 tablespoons butter,
  melted

filling

6 ounces white crabmeat
¾ cup ricotta cheese
finely grated rind of 1 lemon
pinch of crushed red
  pepper

2 tablespoons chopped
  fresh flat-leaf parsley
salt and pepper

> **1** Sift the flour and salt onto a board or work surface, make a well in the center, and add the eggs.

> **2** Stir with a fork to gradually incorporate the flour into the liquid to form a dough.

> **3** Knead for about 5 minutes, until the dough is smooth. Wrap in plastic wrap and let rest for 20 minutes.

> **4** For the filling, stir together the crabmeat, ricotta, lemon rind, crushed red pepper, and parsley. Season with salt and pepper.

213

>5 Roll the dough with a pasta machine or by hand to a thickness of about ⅛ inch and cut into thirty-two 2½-inch squares.

>6 Place a spoonful of the filling in the center of half the squares.

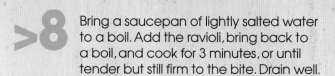

>7 Brush the edges with water and place the remaining squares on top, pressing to seal.

>8 Bring a saucepan of lightly salted water to a boil. Add the ravioli, bring back to a boil, and cook for 3 minutes, or until tender but still firm to the bite. Drain well.

Drizzle the melted butter over the ravioli, sprinkle with pepper, and serve immediately.

vegetables & dairy

tomato soup

serves 4

ingredients
2 tablespoons olive oil
1 large onion, chopped
1 (14½-ounce) can peeled
   Italian tomatoes
1¼ cups chicken stock or
   vegetable stock
1 tablespoon tomato paste
1 teaspoon hot chili sauce
handful of fresh basil leaves
salt and pepper

>1 Heat the oil in a large saucepan over medium heat, add the onion, and sauté, stirring, for 4–5 minutes, until soft.

>2 Add the tomatoes with their can juices, stock, tomato paste, chili sauce, and half the basil leaves.

Serve the soup in warm serving bowls, garnished with the remaining basil leaves.

> 3
Puree with a handheld blender until smooth, then transfer to the pan.

> 4
Stir the soup over medium heat until just boiling, then season with salt and pepper.

minestrone soup

serves 4

ingredients

2 tablespoons olive oil
2 garlic cloves, chopped
2 red onions, chopped
3 ounces prosciutto, sliced
1 red bell pepper, seeded
  and chopped
1 orange bell pepper,
  seeded and chopped
1 (14½-ounce) can diced
  tomatoes
4 cups vegetable stock
1 celery stalk, chopped
1 (15-ounce) can cranberry
  beans, drained and rinsed
1 cup shredded green
  leafy cabbage
½ cup frozen peas
1 tablespoon chopped
  fresh parsley
3 ounces dried vermicelli pasta
salt and pepper
freshly grated Parmesan
  cheese, to serve

>1 Heat the oil in a large saucepan. Add the garlic, onions, and prosciutto and cook over medium heat, stirring, for 3 minutes, until slightly softened.

>2 Add the red bell pepper, orange bell pepper, and diced tomatoes and cook for an additional 2 minutes, stirring. Stir in the stock, then add the celery.

Sprinkle with the Parmesan cheese and serve immediately.

> **>3** Add the beans to the pan with the cabbage, peas, and parsley. Season with salt and pepper. Bring to a boil, then reduce the heat and simmer for 30 minutes.

> **>4** Add the pasta to the pan. Cook according to the pacakge directions. Remove from the heat and ladle into bowls.

cheese & tomato pizza

makes 1 pizza

ingredients

pizza dough

1¾ cups all-purpose flour,
   plus extra for dusting

1 teaspoon salt

1 teaspoon active dry yeast

1 tablespoon olive oil, plus
   extra for oiling

⅓ cup lukewarm water

topping

6 tomatoes, thinly sliced

6 ounces mozzarella
   cheese, thinly sliced

2 tablespoons shredded
   fresh basil

2 tablespoons olive oil

salt and pepper

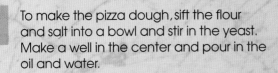

>1 To make the pizza dough, sift the flour and salt into a bowl and stir in the yeast. Make a well in the center and pour in the oil and water.

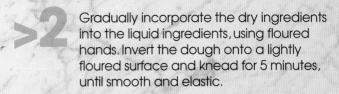

>2 Gradually incorporate the dry ingredients into the liquid ingredients, using floured hands. Invert the dough onto a lightly floured surface and knead for 5 minutes, until smooth and elastic.

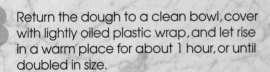

>3 Return the dough to a clean bowl, cover with lightly oiled plastic wrap, and let rise in a warm place for about 1 hour, or until doubled in size.

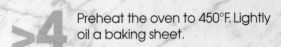

>4 Preheat the oven to 450°F. Lightly oil a baking sheet.

>5 Invert the dough onto a lightly floured surface and punch down into the dough to remove the air. Knead briefly, then roll out into a circle about ¼ inch thick.

>6 Transfer the pizza crust to the prepared baking sheet and push up the edges with your fingers to form a small rim.

>7 For the topping, arrange the tomato and mozzarella slices over the pizza crust.

>8 Season with salt and pepper, sprinkle with basil, and drizzle with oil. Bake in the preheated oven for 20–25 minutes, until golden brown.

Cut into slices and serve immediately.

goat cheese tarts

makes about 12

ingredients

melted butter, for greasing
1½ sheets ready-to-bake
  puff pastry

flour, for dusting
1 egg, beaten
about 3 tablespoons onion
  relish, tomato relish, or salsa

12 ounces goat cheese
  logs, sliced into circles
olive oil, for drizzling
pepper

>1 Preheat the oven to 400°F. Grease 1–2 baking sheets with melted butter.

>2 Transfer the pastry sheet to a lightly floured work surface and roll out lightly to remove any creases, if necessary.

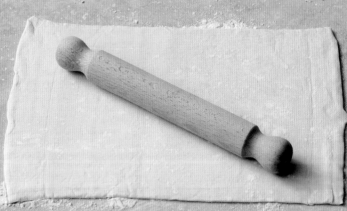

>3 Use a 3-inch pastry cutter to stamp out as many circles as possible.

>4 Place the circles on the baking sheets and press gently about 1 inch from the edge of each with a 2-inch pastry cutter.

>5 Brush the circles with the beaten egg and prick with a fork.

>6 Top each circle with a teaspoon of the relish and a slice of the goat cheese.

>7 Drizzle with oil and season with a little black pepper.

>8 Bake in the preheated oven for 8–10 minutes, or until the pastry is crisp and the cheese is bubbling.

Serve warm.

egg tortilla with feta & corn

serves 3–4

ingredients

3 white round potatoes
2 tablespoons olive oil
1 onion, chopped
1 zucchini, shredded

1¼ cups of canned corn, drained
6 eggs
⅔ cup crumbled, drained feta cheese

salt and pepper
paprika, to garnish

>1 Peel or scrub the potatoes and cut into ½-inch dice.

>2 Cook the potatoes in a saucepan of lightly salted boiling water for 5 minutes, or until just tender. Drain.

>3 Heat the oil in a large, ovenproof skillet over medium heat and sauté the onion for about 5 minutes, until softened.

>4 Stir in the zucchini and potatoes, then cook for 2 minutes. Stir in the corn.

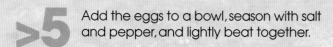

>5 Add the eggs to a bowl, season with salt and pepper, and lightly beat together.

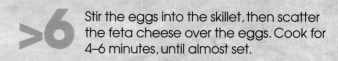

>6 Stir the eggs into the skillet, then scatter the feta cheese over the eggs. Cook for 4–6 minutes, until almost set.

>7 Meanwhile, preheat the broiler to high. Place the tortilla under the preheated broiler for 2–3 minutes, until set and golden brown.

>8 Sprinkle the tortilla with paprika and cut into 4–6 wedges.

232

Serve the tortilla hot or cold.

chili bean stew

serves 4–6

ingredients

2 tablespoons olive oil
1 onion, chopped
2–4 garlic cloves, chopped
2 fresh red chiles, seeded
  and sliced
1 cup canned red kidney
  beans, drained and rinsed
1 cup canned cannellini
  white kidney beans, drained
  and rinsed
1 cup canned chickpeas,
  drained and rinsed
1 tablespoon tomato paste
3–3½ cups vegetable stock
1 red bell pepper, seeded
  and chopped
4 tomatoes, diced
1 cup shelled fresh
  fava beans
1 tablespoon chopped
  fresh cilantro
paprika, to garnish
sour cream, to serve

> **>1** Heat the oil in a large, heavy saucepan with a tight-fitting lid. Add the onion, garlic, and chiles and cook, stirring frequently, for 5 minutes, until soft.

> **>2** Add the red kidney beans, cannellini beans, and chickpeas. Blend the tomato paste with a little of the stock and pour it over the bean mixture, then add the remaining stock.

Garnish with the remaining chopped cilantro and a pinch of paprika and serve topped with spoonfuls of sour cream.

>3 Bring to a boil, then reduce the heat and simmer for 10–15 minutes. Add the red bell pepper, tomatoes, and fava beans.

>4 Simmer for an additional 15–20 minutes, or until all the vegetables are tender. Stir in most of the chopped cilantro.

tacos with chickpea salsa

serves 4

ingredients

2 firm, ripe avocados
1 tablespoon lime juice
1 tomato, diced
1 tablespoon olive oil
1 small onion, sliced

1 (15-ounce) can
chickpeas, drained
and rinsed
1 teaspoon mild chili
powder
8 romaine lettuce leaves

8 tacos
2 tablespoons chopped
fresh cilantro, plus extra
sprigs to garnish
salt and pepper
⅔ cup sour cream, to serve

> **1** Halve, pit, peel, and dice the avocados and toss with the lime juice.

> **2** Stir in the tomato and season well with salt and pepper.

> **3** Heat the oil in a saucepan and sauté the onion for 3–4 minutes, or until golden brown.

> **4** Mash the chickpeas with a fork and stir into the pan with the chili powder. Heat gently, stirring, for 2 minutes.

>5 Divide the lettuce among the tacos. Stir the chopped cilantro into the avocado-and-tomato mixture, then spoon into the tacos.

>6 Add a spoonful of the chickpea mixture to each taco and top with a spoonful of sour cream.

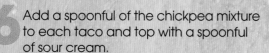

Garnish with cilantro sprigs and
serve immediately.

nut roast

serves 4

ingredients

2 tablespoons olive oil,
  plus extra for brushing
1 large onion, finely
  chopped
1 cup ground almonds
¾ cup finely chopped
  cashew nuts
1 cup fresh whole-wheat
  bread crumbs
½ cup vegetable stock
finely grated rind and juice
  of 1 small lemon
1 tablespoon finely
  chopped rosemary leaves
salt and pepper
fresh rosemary sprigs and
  lemon slices, to garnish

>1 Preheat the oven to 400°F. Brush an 8-inch loaf
pan with oil and line with parchment paper.

>2 Heat the oil in a large saucepan, add
the onion, and saute over medium heat,
stirring, for 3–4 minutes, until soft.

Invert and serve hot, garnished with rosemary sprigs and lemon slices.

>3 Stir in the almonds, cashew nuts, bread crumbs, stock, lemon rind and juice, and rosemary. Season with salt and pepper and stir well to mix.

>4 Press the mixture into the prepared pan, brush with oil, and bake in the preheated oven for 30–35 minutes, until golden brown and firm.

broiled mushrooms & polenta with poached eggs

serves 4

ingredients

8-ouce prepared firm
  polenta (from an Italian
  delicatessen or gourmet
  food supplier)
4 large portobello
mushrooms

4 tablespoons butter
1 garlic clove, crushed
1 tablespoon chopped
  fresh parsley
1 tablespoon snipped fresh
  chives, plus extra to garnish

4 fresh eggs
3½ cups baby spinach
salt and pepper
Parmesan cheese shavings,
  to garnish

>1 Preheat the broiler to high. Cut the polenta into 8 slices and arrange on a baking sheet with the mushrooms.

>2 Melt the butter in a small saucepan with the garlic. Stir in the parsley and chives.

>3 Brush the mushrooms and polenta with the herb butter and season with salt and pepper.

>4 Cook under the preheated broiler for 6–8 minutes, turning once, until the polenta is golden and mushrooms are tender.

>5 Bring a saucepan of water to just under boiling point. Break the eggs carefully into the water.

>6 Poach the eggs for about 3 minutes, until just set. Lift out with a slotted spoon.

>7 Place two slices of polenta on each serving plate and add a small handful of spinach.

>8 Top each with a mushroom, then add a poached egg and spoon the remaining herb butter over the egg.

Garnish with chives and Parmesan cheese
shavings and serve.

mushroom stroganoff

serves 4

ingredients

2 tablespoons butter
1 onion, finely chopped
6½ cups quartered white
    button mushrooms
1 teaspoon tomato paste
1 teaspoon whole-grain
    mustard
⅔ cup crème fraîche
    or sour cream
1 teaspoon paprika,
    plus extra to garnish
salt and pepper
fresh flat-leaf parsley sprigs,
    to garnish

>1 Heat the butter in a large, heavy skillet. Add the onion and cook gently for 5–10 minutes, until soft.

>2 Add the mushrooms to the skillet and sauté, stirring, for a few minutes, until they begin to soften.

Garnish with extra paprika and parsley sprigs and serve immediately.

>3 Stir in the tomato paste and mustard, then add the crème fraîche. Cook gently, stirring continuously, for 5 minutes.

>4 Stir in the paprika and season with salt and pepper.

mushroom & cauliflower casserole

serves 4

ingredients
1 cauliflower, cut into florets
4 tablespoons butter
1½ cups sliced white button
 mushrooms
salt and pepper

topping
1 cup dry bread crumbs
2 tablespoons grated
 Parmesan cheese

1 teaspoon dried oregano
1 teaspoon dried parsley
2 tablespoons butter

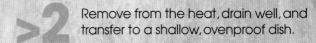

>**1** Bring a large saucepan of lightly salted water to a boil. Add the cauliflower and cook for 3 minutes.

>**2** Remove from the heat, drain well, and transfer to a shallow, ovenproof dish.

>**3** Preheat the oven to 450°F. Melt the butter in a small skillet over medium heat. Add the mushrooms, stir, and cook gently for 3 minutes.

>**4** Remove from the heat and spoon on top of the cauliflower. Season with salt and pepper.

>5 Combine the bread crumbs, Parmesan cheese, and herbs in a small mixing bowl, then sprinkle the mixture over the vegetables.

>6 Dice the butter and place over the bread crumb mixture. Bake in the preheated oven for 15 minutes, or until the topping is golden brown.

Serve straight from the ovenproof dish.

risotto with peas & gorgonzola

serves 4

ingredients

2 tablespoons olive oil
2 tablespoons butter
1 onion, finely chopped
1 garlic clove, finely
  chopped
2 cups risotto rice
⅔ cup dry white wine
5½ cups hot
  vegetable stock
2⅓ cups frozen peas
1 cup crumbled
  Gorgonzola cheese
  or other blue cheese
2 tablespoons chopped
  fresh mint
salt and pepper

>1 Heat the oil and butter in a deep saucepan. Add the onion and cook, stirring frequently, for 3–4 minutes, until softened.

>2 Add the garlic and rice and mix to coat in the butter and oil. Cook, stirring continuously, for 2–3 minutes, or until the grains are translucent. Add the wine and cook, stirring continuously, for 1 minute, until reduced.

Serve the risotto immediately.

>3 Gradually add the hot stock, a ladleful at a time. Cook, stirring, for 15 minutes, then stir in the peas and cook for an additional 5 minutes, until the liquid is absorbed and the rice is creamy.

>4 Remove from the heat. Stir in the Gorgonzola cheese and mint, then season with salt and pepper.

cannelloni with spinach & ricotta

serves 4

ingredients
melted butter, for greasing
12 dried cannelloni tubes,
  each about 3 inches long
salt and pepper

filling
½ (10-ounce) package
  frozen spinach, thawed
  and drained
½ cup ricotta cheese
1 egg

3 tablespoons grated
  pecorino cheese
pinch of freshly grated
  nutmeg
salt and pepper

cheese sauce
2 tablespoons butter
2 tablespoons
  all-purpose flour
2½ cups hot milk
¾ cup shredded
  Swiss cheese
salt and pepper

> **1** Preheat the oven to 350°F. Grease a rectangular ovenproof dish with the melted butter.

> **2** Bring a large saucepan of lightly salted water to a boil. Add the cannelloni tubes, bring back to a boil. and cook according to the package directions, until nearly tender. Drain and rinse, then spread out on a clean dish towel.

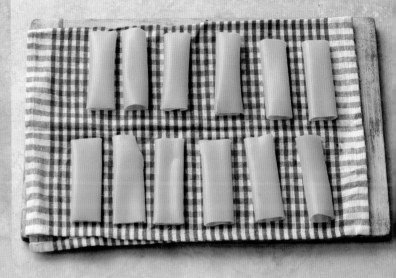

> **3** For the filling, put the spinach and ricotta into a food processor and process briefly until combined. Add the egg and pecorino cheese and process to a smooth paste. Transfer to a bowl, add the nutmeg, and season with salt and pepper.

> **4** Spoon the filling into a pastry bag fitted with a ½-inch nozzle. Carefully open a cannelloni tube and pipe in a little of the filling. Place the filled tube in the prepared dish and repeat.

>5 For the cheese sauce, melt the butter in a saucepan. Add the flour to the butter and cook over low heat, stirring continuously, for 1 minute.

>6 Remove from the heat and gradually stir in the hot milk. Return to the heat and bring to a boil, stirring continuously. Simmer over low heat, stirring frequently, for 10 minutes, until thickened and smooth.

>7 Remove from the heat, stir in the Swiss cheese, and season with salt and pepper.

>8 Spoon the cheese sauce over the filled cannelloni. Cover the dish with aluminum foil and bake in the preheated oven for 20–25 minutes.

Serve immediately.

pappardelle with cherry tomatoes & arugula

serves 4

ingredients
1 pound dried pappardelle
2 tablespoons olive oil
1 garlic clove, chopped
2⅓ cups halved cherry
 tomatoes
4 cups arugula
8 ounces mozzarella,
 chopped
salt and pepper
grated Parmesan cheese,
 to serve

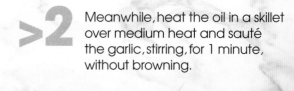

>1 Bring a large saucepan of lightly salted water to a boil. Add the pasta, bring back to a boil, and cook according to the package directions, or until tender but still firm to the bite.

>2 Meanwhile, heat the oil in a skillet over medium heat and sauté the garlic, stirring, for 1 minute, without browning.

Serve the pasta in wide dishes, sprinkled with Parmesan cheese.

>3 Add the tomatoes, season well with salt and pepper, and cook gently for 2–3 minutes, until softened.

>4 Drain the pasta and stir into the skillet. Add the arugula and mozzarella, then stir until the leaves wilt.

macaroni & cheese

serves 4

ingredients

8 ounces dried
  macaroni pasta
2½ cups milk
½ teaspoon grated nutmeg

4 tablespoons butter, plus
  extra for cooking the pasta
½ cup all-purpose flour
1¾ cups shredded
  cheddar cheese or
  American cheese

¾ cup freshly grated
  Parmesan cheese
salt and pepper

>1 Bring a large saucepan of lightly salted water to a boil. Add the pasta and cook according to the package directions, or until tender but still firm to the bite. Remove from the heat and drain. Add a small pat of butter, return to the saucepan, and cover to keep warm.

>2 Put the milk and nutmeg into a saucepan over low heat and heat until warm, but do not bring to a boil.

>3 Melt the butter in a heavy saucepan over low heat, then add the flour and stir to make a paste. Cook gently for 2 minutes.

>4 Add the milk a little at a time, beating it into the paste, then cook for about 10–15 minutes to make a sauce.

261

>5 Add 1 cup of the cheddar cheese and ½ cup of the Parmesan cheese and stir through until they melt. Season with salt and pepper and remove from the heat.

>6 Preheat the broiler to high. Put the macaroni into a shallow, heatproof dish, then pour the sauce over the pasta.

>7 Sprinkle the remaining cheese over the top and place the dish under the broiler.

>8 Broil until the cheese begins to brown.

Serve immediately.

spicy pasta

serves 4

ingredients

⅓ cup extra virgin olive oil
8 plum tomatoes, diced
⅔ cup dry white wine
1 tablespoon tomato paste
2 fresh red chiles
2 garlic cloves, finely
  chopped
¼ cup chopped fresh
  flat-leaf parsley
1 pound penne
salt and pepper
fresh pecorino cheese
  shavings, to garnish

1 To make the sauce, heat the oil in a skillet over high heat until almost smoking. Add the tomatoes and cook, stirring frequently, for 2–3 minutes.

>2 Reduce the heat to low and cook for about 20 minutes. Season with salt and pepper. Using a wooden spoon, press through a nonmetallic strainer into a saucepan.

Sprinkle with the remaining parsley, garnish with cheese shavings, and serve immediately.

>3 Add the wine, tomato paste, whole chiles, and garlic to the skillet and bring to a boil. Reduce the heat and simmer gently, then remove the chiles. Check and adjust the seasoning, adding the chiles back in for a hotter sauce, then stir in half the parsley.

>4 Meanwhile, bring a large saucepan of lightly salted water to a boil. Add the pasta, bring back to a boil, and cook according to the package directions, or until tender but still firm to the bite. Add the sauce to the pasta and toss to coat.

eggplant gratin

serves 2

ingredients

¼ cup olive oil
2 onions, finely chopped
2 garlic cloves, finely chopped
2 eggplants, thickly sliced

3 tablespoons chopped fresh flat-leaf parsley, plus extra sprigs to garnish
½ teaspoon dried thyme

1 (14½-ounce) can diced tomatoes
1½ cups shredded mozzarella cheese,

⅓ cup freshly grated Parmesan cheese
salt and pepper

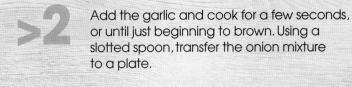

>1 Heat the oil in a dutch oven or flameproof casserole over medium heat. Add the onions and cook for 5 minutes, or until soft.

>2 Add the garlic and cook for a few seconds, or until just beginning to brown. Using a slotted spoon, transfer the onion mixture to a plate.

>3 Add the eggplant slices to the pot, in batches, and cook until lightly browned. Transfer to another plate.

>4 Preheat the oven to 400°F. Arrange a layer of eggplant slices in the bottom of the pot or a shallow, ovenproof dish.

267

>5 Sprinkle with some of the parsley and thyme, and season with salt and pepper.

>6 Add layers of onion, tomatoes, and mozzarella cheese, sprinkling with parsley, and thyme and seasoning with salt and pepper for each layer.

>7 Continue layering, finishing with a layer of eggplant slices.

>8 Sprinkle with the Parmesan cheese and bake, uncovered, in the preheated oven for 20–30 minutes, or until the top is golden and the eggplants are tender.

Serve hot, garnished with parsley sprigs.

tomato ratatouille

serves 4

ingredients

1 teaspoon olive oil
1 onion, cut into small
   wedges
2–4 garlic cloves, chopped
1 small eggplant, chopped
1 red bell pepper, seeded
   and chopped
1 yellow bell pepper,
   seeded and chopped
1 zucchini, chopped
2 tablespoons tomato paste
3 tablespoons water
1½ cups halved white
   button mushrooms,
2 tomatoes, diced
pepper
1 tablespoon shredded
   fresh basil, to garnish
2 tablespoons grated
   Parmesan cheese, to serve

> **>1** Heat the oil in a heavy saucepan. Add the onion, garlic, and eggplant and cook, stirring frequently, for 3 minutes.

> **>2** Add the red and yellow bell peppers and the zucchini.

Divide the ratatouille among warm dishes, garnish with shredded basil, and serve with Parmesan cheese.

>3 Mix together the tomato paste and water in a small bowl and stir into the pan. Bring to a boil, cover, reduce the heat to a simmer, and cook for 10 minutes.

>4 Add the mushrooms and tomatoes, season with pepper, and continue to simmer for 12–15 minutes, stirring occasionally, until the vegetables are tender.

tofu stir-fry

serves 4

ingredients

2 tablespoons sunflower oil
1½ cups diced firm tofu
3 cups coarsely chopped
  bok choy

1 garlic clove, chopped
¼ cup sweet chili sauce
2 tablespoons light soy
  sauce

>1 Heat 1 tablespoon of the oil in a wok.

>2 Add the tofu to the wok, in batches, and stir-fry for 2–3 minutes, until golden. Remove and set aside.

>3 Add the bok choy to the wok and stir-fry for a few seconds, until tender and wilted. Remove and set aside.

>4 Heat the remaining oil in the wok, then add the garlic and stir-fry for 30 seconds.

>5 Stir in the chili sauce and soy sauce and bring to a boil.

>6 Return the tofu and bok choy to the wok and toss gently until coated in the sauce.

Transfer to individual dishes and serve immediately.

jamaican rice & peas with tofu

serves 4

ingredients

8 ounces firm tofu

2 tablespoons chopped fresh thyme, plus extra sprigs to garnish

2 tablespoons olive oil

1 onion, sliced

1 garlic clove, crushed

1 small fresh red chile, chopped

1¾ cups vegetable stock

1 cup basmati rice

¼ cup coconut cream or coconut milk

1 (15-ounce) can red kidney beans, drained and rinsed

salt and pepper

>1 Cut the tofu into bite-size cubes. Toss with half the chopped thyme and season with salt and pepper.

>2 Heat 1 tablespoon of the oil in a skillet and sauté the tofu, stirring occasionally, for 2 minutes. Remove and keep warm.

>3 Sauté the onion in the remaining oil, stirring, for 3–4 minutes.

>4 Stir in the garlic, chile, and the remaining chopped thyme, then add the stock and bring to a boil.

>5 Stir in the rice, then reduce the heat, cover, and simmer for 12–15 minutes, until the rice is tender.

>6 Stir in the coconut cream and beans, season with salt and pepper, and cook gently for 2–3 minutes.

Spoon the tofu over the rice and serve hot, garnished with thyme sprigs.

desserts

tiramisu

serves 6

ingredients

4 egg yolks
½ cup granulated sugar
1 teaspoon vanilla extract

2 cups mascarpone cheese
2 egg whites
¾ cup strong black coffee

½ cup rum or brandy
24 ladyfingers
2 tablespoons unsweetened
  cocoa powder

2 tablespoons finely grated
  semisweet dark chocolate

>**1** Beat the egg yolks with the sugar and vanilla extract in a heatproof bowl set over a saucepan of barely simmering water.

>**2** When the mixture is pale and the whisk leaves a ribbon trail when lifted, remove the bowl from the heat and set aside to cool. Beat occasionally to prevent a skin from forming.

>**3** When the egg yolk mixture is cool, beat in the mascarpone cheese until thoroughly combined.

>**4** Beat the egg whites in a separate, spotlessly clean bowl until they form soft peaks, then gently fold them into the mascarpone mixture.

> **5** Combine the coffee and rum in a shallow dish. Briefly dip 8 of the ladyfingers in the mixture, then arrange in the bottom of a serving dish.

> **6** Spoon one-third of the mascarpone mixture on top, spreading it out evenly. Repeat the layers twice, finishing with the mascarpone mixture. Chill for at least 1 hour.

To serve, sift the cocoa evenly over the top
and sprinkle with the chocolate.

285

mini apple crisps

serves 4

ingredients

2 large Granny Smith
  apples, peeled, cored,
  and chopped
3 tablespoons maple syrup
juice of ½ lemon
½ teaspoon ground allspice
4 tablespoons
  unsalted butter
1 cup rolled oats
3 tablespoons packed
  light brown sugar

>1 Preheat the oven to 425°F. Place a baking sheet in the oven to heat. Put the apples into a saucepan and stir in the maple syrup, lemon juice, and allspice.

>2 Bring to a boil over high heat, then reduce the heat to medium, cover the pan, and cook for 5 minutes, or until almost tender.

Serve the crisps warm.

> **3** Meanwhile, melt the butter in a separate saucepan, then remove from the heat and stir in the oats and sugar.

> **4** Divide the apples amoung four 1-cup ovenproof dishes. Sprinkle the oat mixture over the apples. Place on the baking sheet in the preheated oven and bake for 10 minutes, until lightly browned and bubbling.

strawberry cheesecake

serves 8

ingredients

crust
4 tablespoons unsalted
  butter
2 cups crushed graham
  crackers
¾ cup chopped walnuts

filling
2 cups mascarpone cheese
2 eggs, beaten
3 tablespoons granulated
  sugar

8 ounces white chocolate,
  broken into pieces
1 pint strawberries, hulled
  and quartered

topping
¾ cup mascarpone cheese
2 ounces white chocolate
  shavings
4 strawberries, halved

>1 Preheat the oven to 300°F. Melt the butter in a saucepan over low heat and stir in the crushed graham crackers and walnuts.

>2 Spoon into a 9-inch springform cake pan and press evenly over the bottom with the back of a spoon. Set aside.

>3 To make the filling, beat the mascarpone cheese in a bowl until smooth, then beat in the eggs and sugar.

>4 Melt the white chocolate in a heatproof bowl set over a saucepan of gently simmering water, stirring until smooth. Remove from the heat and let cool slightly, then stir into the cheese mixture. Stir in the strawberries.

289

>5 Spoon the batter into the cake pan, spread evenly, and smooth the surface. Bake in the preheated oven for 1 hour, or until just firm.

>6 Turn off the oven and keep the cheesecake inside it with the door slightly open until completely cold. Transfer to a serving plate.

Spread the mascarpone cheese on top, decorate with the chocolate shavings and the strawberry halves, and serve.

lemon meringue pie

serves 6–8

ingredients

pie dough

1¼ cups all-purpose flour,
plus extra for dusting

6 tablespoons butter,
cut into small pieces,
plus extra for greasing

¼ cup confectioners' sugar,
sifted

finely grated rind of
½ lemon

½ egg yolk, beaten

1½ tablespoons whole milk

filling

3 tablespoons cornstarch

1¼ cups water

juice and grated rind of
2 lemons

1 cup superfine sugar
or granulated sugar

2 eggs, separated

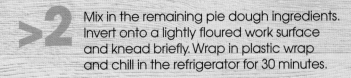

>1 To make the pie dough, sift the flour into a bowl. Rub in the butter with your fingertips until the mixture resembles fine bread crumbs.

>2 Mix in the remaining pie dough ingredients. Invert onto a lightly floured work surface and knead briefly. Wrap in plastic wrap and chill in the refrigerator for 30 minutes.

>3 Preheat the oven to 350°F. Grease an 8-inch round tart pan. Roll out the dough to a thickness of ¼ inch, then use to line the pan.

>4 Prick all over with a fork, line with parchment paper, and fill with pie weights or dried beans. Bake in the preheated oven for 15 minutes.

>5 Remove the pastry shell from the oven and take out the paper and weights. Reduce the oven temperature to 300°F.

>6 To make the filling, mix the cornstarch with a little of the water to form a paste. Put the remaining water in a saucepan. Stir in the lemon juice, lemon rind, and cornstarch paste.

>7 Bring to a boil, stirring. Cook for 2 minutes. Let cool slightly. Stir in 1/3 cup of the superfine sugar and the egg yolks. Pour into the pastry shell.

>8 Beat the egg whites until stiff. Gradually beat in the remaining superfine sugar and spread over the pie. Return to the oven and bake for an additional 40 minutes.

Remove from the oven, let cool, and serve.

chocolate mousse

serves 4–6

ingredients

8 ounces semisweet dark
  chocolate, chopped
2 tablespoons brandy,
  Grand Marnier or
  Cointreau
¼ cup water
2 tablespoons unsalted
  butter, diced
3 extra-large eggs,
  separated
¼ teaspoon cream
  of tartar
¼ cup granulated sugar
½ cup heavy cream

> **>1** Put the chocolate, brandy, and water in a heatproof bowl set over a small saucepan over low heat and stir until smooth. Remove from the heat. Beat in the butter and then the egg yolks, one at a time, until blended. Cool slightly.

> **>2** Meanwhile, beat the egg whites in a clean bowl until holding soft peaks. Sprinkle the cream of tartar over the egg whites, then gradually add the sugar, beating until holding stiff peaks.

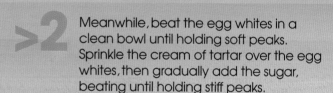

Spoon the mousse into individual bowls. Cover with plastic wrap and chill for at least 3 hours before serving.

>3 Beat several tablespoons of the beaten egg white into the chocolate mixture to loosen it.

>4 Whip the cream until holding soft peaks. Spoon the cream over the chocolate mixture, then add the remaining egg whites mixture. Use a spatula to fold the chocolate into the cream and egg whites mixture.

panna cotta with spiced plums

serves 4

ingredients
panna cotta
4 gelatin leaves
1¼ cups whole milk
1 cup mascarpone

½ cup granulated sugar
1 vanilla bean, halved
  lengthwise

spiced plums
8 red plums, halved
  and pitted
3 tablespoons honey
1 cinnamon stick

thinly pared strip of
  orange zest
1 tablespoon balsamic
  vinegar

>1 Soak the gelatin leaves in ¼ cup of the milk for 10 minutes.

>2 Place the remaining milk, the mascarpone cheese, sugar, and vanilla bean in a saucepan and heat gently, stirring until smooth, then bring to a boil.

>3 Remove from the heat, discard the vanilla bean, and add the gelatin mixture, stirring until completely dissolved.

>4 Pour into four 1-cup individual dessert molds. Let chill in the refrigerator until set.

>5 Place the plums, honey, cinnamon stick, orange zest, and vinegar in a saucepan. Cover and cook gently for 10 minutes, or until the plums are tender.

>6 Dip the bottom of each mold quickly in hot water and turn out onto a serving plate.

Serve the panna cotta with the spiced plums
on the side.

stuffed peaches
with amaretto

serves 4

ingredients

4 tablespoons
  unsalted butter
4 peaches
2 tablespoons packed
  light brown sugar
1 cup crushed amaretti
  cookies
2 tablespoons amaretto
½ cup light cream,
  to serve

> **1** Preheat the oven to 350°F. Using 1 tablespoon of the butter, grease an ovenproof dish, large enough to hold 8 peach halves in a single layer.

> **2** Halve the peaches and remove and discard the pits.

Pour over the amaretto and serve hot with cream.

>3 Beat together the remaining butter and the sugar in a bowl until creamy. Add the cookie crumbs and mix well.

>4 Arrange the peach halves, cut side up, in the prepared ovenproof dish and fill the cavities with the cookie mixture. Bake in the preheated oven for 20–25 minutes, or until tender.

pineapple dessert

serves 6

ingredients

1 pineapple
¼ cup golden raisins
2 tablespoons raisins
¼ cup maple syrup

¼ cup white rum
1 egg yolk
1 tablespoon cornstarch
½ teaspoon vanilla extract

¼ teaspoon ground ginger
2 egg whites
2 tablespoons packed
  brown sugar

>1 Preheat the oven to 475°F. Cut off the leafy top and the bottom of the pineapple and discard.

>2 Stand the pineapple upright and slice off the skin. Remove any remaining "eyes" with the tip of a small sharp knife. Cut in half lengthwise and remove the hard woody core, then slice the flesh.

>3 Arrange the pineapple slices in a large ovenproof dish and sprinkle with the golden raisins and raisins. Drizzle with half the maple syrup and half the rum. Bake in the preheated oven for 5 minutes.

>4 Meanwhile, mix the remaining maple syrup and rum with the egg yolk, cornstarch, vanilla extract, and ginger in a bowl.

>5 Beat the egg whites in a separate bowl until soft peaks form. Stir 2 tablespoons of the egg white into the egg yolk mixture, then fold the remaining egg yolk mixture into the egg whites.

>6 Spread the topping over the hot pineapple, sprinkle the sugar over the top, and bake in the preheated oven for 5 minutes, or until golden brown.

coconut pancakes with pineapple

serves 4

ingredients

1¼ cups all-purpose flour
2 tablespoons granulated
 sugar
2 eggs

1¾ cups coconut milk
1 medium pineapple
peanut oil, for frying

toasted, shredded dried
 coconut, to decorate
half-and-half flavored with a
 few drops coconut extract,
 to serve

> **1** Sift the flour and sugar into a bowl and make a well in the center.

> **2** Add the eggs and coconut milk to the well and stir into the flour, then beat to a smooth, bubbly batter.

> **3** Stand the pineapple upright and slice off the skin. Remove any remaining "eyes" with the tip of a small knife. Cut in half lengthwise and remove the hard woody core. Cut the flesh into chunks.

> **4** Heat a small amount of oil in a heavy skillet and pour in a little batter, swirling to cover the skillet.

>5 Cook the thin pancake over high heat until set and golden underneath.

>6 Toss or turn the pancake and cook until golden on the other side.

>7 Repeat with the remaining batter to make 8–10 pancakes, stacking alternately with wax paper between while making the rest.

>8 Fill the pancakes with pieces of pineapple and fold into fan shapes to serve.

Sprinkle the pancakes with toasted shreds of coconut and serve drizzled with the coconut-flavored cream.

raspberry croissant desserts

serves 4

ingredients

2 tablespoons unsalted
   butter, melted
4 croissants

2 cups fresh raspberries
¼ cup maple syrup
1½ cups whole milk

2 extra-large eggs, beaten
1 teaspoon vanilla extract
freshly grated nutmeg,
   for sprinkling

>1 Preheat the oven to 425°F. Place a baking sheet on the middle shelf.

>2 Brush four 1½-cup ramekins (individual ceramic dishes) with half the butter.

>3 Chop the croissants into bite-size chunks. Mix with the raspberries and divide among the dishes.

>4 Spoon 1 tablespoon of the maple syrup over the contents of each dish.

>5 Heat the milk until almost boiling, then quickly beat in the eggs and vanilla extract.

>6 Pour the milk mixture evenly over the dishes, pressing the croissants down lightly.

>7 Drizzle with the remaining butter and sprinkle a little nutmeg over each dish.

>8 Place the dishes on the baking sheet and bake in the preheated oven for about 20 minutes, until lightly set.

ricotta tart with chocolate & walnuts

serves 6

ingredients

½ cup granulated sugar
1 stick unsalted butter,
  softened
2 egg yolks
finely grated rind of 1 lemon
2 cups all-purpose flour

filling

4 ounces semisweet
  dark chocolate,
  broken into pieces
1 cup ricotta cheese
¼ cup confectioners' sugar,
  plus extra for dusting

2 tablespoons dark rum
1 teaspoon vanilla extract
¾ cup finely chopped
  walnuts

> **1** Preheat the oven to 350°F. Place the granulated sugar, butter, egg yolks, and lemon rind in a bowl and beat well to mix evenly.

> **2** Add the flour and work the mixture with your fingers to make a smooth dough.

> **3** Wrap the dough in plastic wrap and let rest at room temperature for about 10 minutes.

> **4** Melt the chocolate in a heatproof bowl set over a saucepan of hot water.

Mix together the ricotta cheese, confectioners' sugar, rum, vanilla extract, and walnuts. Stir in the melted chocolate, mixing evenly.

Roll out two-thirds of the dough and press into the bottom and sides of a 9-inch loose-bottom tart pan.

 Spoon the ricotta mixture into the pie shell, smoothing level.

Roll out the remaining dough, cut into strips, and arrange over the tart to form a lattice. Place on a baking sheet and bake in the preheated oven for 35–40 minutes, until firm and golden.

Serve the tart warm, dusted with confectioners' sugar.

mini fig tarts

serves 4

ingredients

1 sheet ready-to-bake
  puff pastry
all-purpose flour,
  for dusting

8 fresh ripe figs
1 tablespoon
  granulated sugar

½ teaspoon ground
  cinnamon
milk, for brushing
vanilla ice cream, to serve

>1 Preheat the oven to 375°F. Roll out the pastry on a lightly floured surface to a thickness of ¼ inch.

>2 Using a saucer as a guide, cut out four 6-inch circles and place on a baking sheet.

>3 Use a sharp knife to score a line halfway through each pastry circle about ½ inch from the outer edge. Prick the center all over with a fork.

>4 Slice the figs into quarters and arrange 8 quarters over the center of each pastry circle.

>5 Mix together the sugar and cinnamon and sprinkle over the figs.

>6 Brush the edges of the pastry with milk and bake in the preheated oven for 15–20 minutes, until risen and golden brown.

Serve the mini tarts warm with ice cream.

coconut ice cream

serves 4

ingredients
1¾ cups coconut milk
⅔ cup granulated sugar
⅔ cup light cream
rind of ½ lime, finely grated
2 tablespoons lime juice
curls of lime zest, to
  decorate

> **1** Place half the coconut milk and the sugar in a saucepan and stir over medium heat until the sugar has dissolved.

> **2** Remove from the heat and stir in the remaining coconut milk, cream, lime rind, and lime juice. Let cool completely.

Top with curled shreds of lime zest and serve.

>**3** Transfer to a freezer-proof container and freeze for 2 hours, beating with a fork at hourly intervals.

>**4** Serve the ice cream scooped into glasses or bowls.

butterscotch, mango
& ginger sundaes

serves 4

ingredients

½ cup firmly packed light
  brown sugar
½ cup dark corn syrup
4 tablespoons unsalted
  butter

½ cup heavy cream
½ teaspoon vanilla extract
1 large, ripe mango
8 gingersnaps

1 quart vanilla ice cream
2 tablespoons coarsely
  chopped almonds,
  toasted

> **1** To make the butterscotch sauce, melt the sugar, corn syrup, and butter in a small saucepan and simmer for 3 minutes, stirring, until smooth.

> **2** Stir in the cream and vanilla extract, then remove from the heat.

> **3** Peel and pit the mango and cut into ½-inch cubes.

> **4** Place the gingersnaps in a plastic food bag and crush lightly with a rolling pin.

327

>5 Place half the mango in four sundae glasses and top each with a scoop of the ice cream.

>6 Spoon over a little butterscotch sauce and sprinkle with the crushed gingersnaps. Repeat with the remaining glasses.

Sprinkle some of the almonds over the top of each sundae and serve immediately.

zabaglione

serves 4

ingredients
4 egg yolks
⅓ cup graunlated sugar
⅓ cup Marsala wine
amaretti cookies, to serve

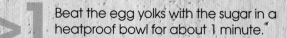 **>1** Beat the egg yolks with the sugar in a
heatproof bowl for about 1 minute.

 >2 Gently beat in the Marsala.

Serve with amaretti cookies.

>3 Set the bowl over a saucepan of barely simmering water and beat vigorously for 10–15 minutes, until thick, creamy and foamy.

>4 Immediately pour into serving glasses.

331

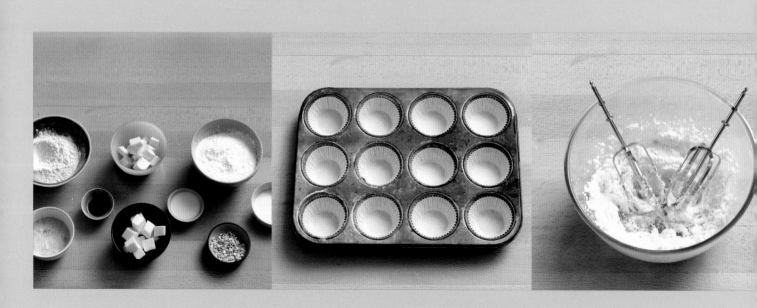

baking

frosted chocolate cake

serves 8

ingredients

1¼ cups all-purpose flour
¼ cup unsweetened
 cocoa powder
1 cup granulated sugar
1 tablespoon baking
 powder

1½ sticks unsalted butter, at
 room temperature, plus
 extra for greasing
3 eggs, beaten
1 teaspoon vanilla extract
2 tablespoons whole milk

frosting

1 stick unsalted butter, at
 room temperature
1⅔ cups confectioners'
 sugar

2 tablespoons unsweetened
 cocoa powder
1 teaspoon vanilla extract

> **1** Preheat the oven to 350°F. Grease and line the bottom and sides of two 8-inch cake pans.

> **2** Sift the flour, cocoa, sugar, and baking powder into a large bowl and make a well in the center.

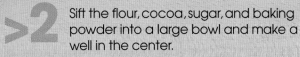

> **3** Beat the butter until soft. Add to the dry ingredients with the eggs, vanilla extract, and milk. Beat lightly with a wooden spoon until just smooth.

> **4** Spoon the batter into the prepared pans, smoothing with a spatula. Bake in the preheated oven for 25–30 minutes, until risen and firm.

>5 Let the cakes cool in the pans for 2–3 minutes, then invert onto a wire rack and let cool completely.

>6 To make the frosting, beat the butter until smooth and fluffy. Sift the confectioners' sugar with the cocoa and beat into the butter until smooth.

>7 Stir in the vanilla extract with enough hot water to mix to a soft spreading consistency.

>8 When the cakes are cold, sandwich them together with half the frosting, then spread the remainder over the top, swirling with a spatula.

Cut into slices and serve.

classic cherry cake

serves 8

ingredients

1¼ cups quartered candied cherries

1 cup almond meal (ground almonds)

1⅔ cups all-purpose flour

1 teaspoon baking powder

1¾ sticks unsalted butter, plus extra for greasing

1 cup granulated sugar

3 extra-large eggs

finely grated rind and juice of 1 lemon

6 sugar cubes, crushed

> **1** Preheat the oven to 350°F. Grease and line an 8-inch round cake pan.

> **2** Stir together the cherries, almonds, and 1 tablespoon of the flour. Sift the remaining flour into a separate bowl with the baking powder.

> **3** Cream together the butter and sugar until light and fluffy. Gradually add the eggs, beating hard, until evenly mixed.

> **4** Add the flour mixture and fold lightly and evenly into the creamed mixture with a metal spoon. Add the cherry mixture. Fold in evenly, then fold in the lemon rind and juice.

> **5** Spoon the batter into the prepared pan and sprinkle with the crushed sugar cubes. Bake in the preheated oven for 1–1¼ hours, or until risen and golden brown and shrinking from the sides of the pan.

> **6** Let cool in the pan for about 15 minutes, then invert onto a wire rack to cool completely.

Cut into slices and serve as
a midmorning treat.

pineapple & coconut bundt cake

serves 12

ingredients

1 (15½-ounce) can
  pineapple slices, drained
1 stick unsalted butter,
  softened, plus extra for
  greasing

1 cup granulated sugar
2 eggs and 1 egg yolk,
  beaten together
2 cups all-purpose flour
1 teaspoon baking powder

½ teaspoon baking soda
½ cup flaked dried coconut

frosting
¾ cup cream cheese
1⅓ cups confectioners'
  sugar

>1 Preheat the oven to 350°F. Grease a 9½-inch tube pan.

>2 Place the pineapple slices in a blender or food processor and process briefly until just crushed.

>3 Beat together the butter and granulated sugar until light and fluffy.

>4 Gradually beat in the eggs until combined.

5 Sift together the flour, baking powder, and baking soda over the egg mixture, then fold in. Fold in the crushed pineapple and the coconut.

 6 Spoon the batter into the prepared pan and bake in the preheated oven for 25 minutes, until a toothpick inserted into the center comes out clean.

>7 Let cool in the pan for 10 minutes before turning out onto a wire rack to cool completely.

 8 To make the frosting, mix together the cream cheese and confectioners' sugar and spread over the cooled cake.

banana coconut loaf cake

makes 1 loaf

ingredients

2 cups all-purpose flour

1½ teaspoons baking
powder

1 cup granulated sugar

¾ cup flaked dried coconut

2 eggs

⅓ cup sunflower oil, plus
extra for greasing

2 ripe bananas, mashed

½ cup sour cream

1 teaspoon vanilla extract

shredded dried coconut,
toasted, to decorate

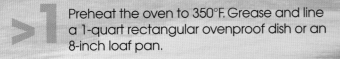

>1 Preheat the oven to 350°F. Grease and line a 1-quart rectangular ovenproof dish or an 8-inch loaf pan.

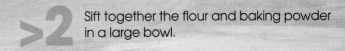

>2 Sift together the flour and baking powder in a large bowl.

>3 Stir in the sugar and coconut.

>4 Beat together the eggs, oil, bananas, cream, and vanilla extract in a large bowl.

347

>5 Stir into the dry ingredients, mixing until evenly combined.

>6 Spoon the batter into the prepared dish, leveling with a spatula.

>7 Bake in the preheated oven for about 1 hour, or until risen, firm, and golden brown.

>8 Cool in the dish for 15 minutes, then invert onto a wire rack to cool completely.

Decorate with shreds of coconut and serve.

vanilla-frosted cupcakes

makes 12 cupcakes

ingredients

1 stick salted butter,
  softened
½ cup granulated sugar
2 eggs, lightly beaten

1 cup all-purpose flour
  plus 1½ teaspoons
  baking powder
1 tablespoon milk
1 tablespoon sprinkles

frosting
1½ sticks unsalted butter,
  softened
1 teaspoon vanilla extract

2¼ cups confectioners'
  sugar, sifted

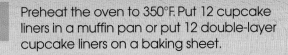
>1 Preheat the oven to 350°F. Put 12 cupcake liners in a muffin pan or put 12 double-layer cupcake liners on a baking sheet.

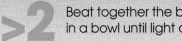
>2 Beat together the butter and sugar in a bowl until light and fluffy.

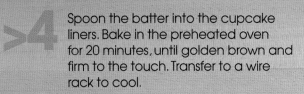
>3 Gradually beat in the eggs. Sift in the flour and baking powder and fold in with the milk.

>4 Spoon the batter into the cupcake liners. Bake in the preheated oven for 20 minutes, until golden brown and firm to the touch. Transfer to a wire rack to cool.

5 To make the frosting, put the butter and vanilla extract in a bowl and beat until pale and soft. Gradually add the confectioners' sugar, beating well after each addition.

 6 Spoon the frosting into a large pastry bag fitted with a medium star-shape tip and pipe swirls of frosting on the top of each cupcake.

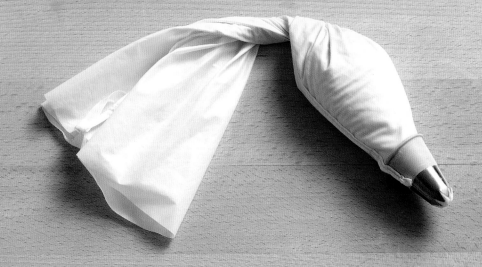

chocolate butterfly cupcakes

makes 12 cupcakes

ingredients

1 stick margarine, softened
⅔ cup granulated sugar
1¼ cups all-purpose flour,
  plus 1¾ teaspoons baking
  powder, sifted together

2 extra-large eggs
2 tablespoons unsweetened
  cocoa powder
1 ounce semisweet dark
  chocolate, melted

lemon buttercream
1 stick unsalted butter,
  softened
1¾ cups confectioners'
  sugar, sifted, plus extra
  for dusting

grated rind of ½ lemon
1 tablespoon lemon juice

>1 Preheat the oven to 350°F. Place 12 cupcake liners in a shallow muffin pan.

>2 Place the margarine, granulated sugar, flour and baking powder, eggs, and cocoa powder in a large bowl and beat until the just smooth. Beat in the melted chocolate.

>3 Spoon the mixture into the cupcake liners, filling them three-quarters full.

>4 Bake in the preheated oven for 15 minutes, or until well risen. Remove from the oven and place on a wire rack to cool.

>5 To make the buttercream, place the butter in a mixing bowl and beat until fluffy. Gradually add in the confectioners' sugar, lemon rind, and lemon juice, beating well with each addition.

>6 Cut the top off each cake, using a serrated knife. Cut each cake top in half. Spread the lemon buttercream over the cut surface of each cake and push the two pieces of cake top into the frosting to form wings.

Dust with confectioners' sugar and serve.

low-fat blueberry muffins

makes 12 muffins

ingredients

1¾ cups all-purpose flour
1 teaspoon baking soda
¼ teaspoon salt
1 teaspoon ground allspice

½ cup granulated sugar
3 extra-large egg whites
3 tablespoons low-fat
 margarine

⅔ cup thick low-fat plain
 yogurt or blueberry-
 flavored yogurt
1 teaspoon vanilla extract
½ cup fresh blueberries

>**1** Preheat the oven to 375°F. Place 12 muffin cups in a shallow muffin pan.

>**2** Sift the flour, baking soda, salt, and half the allspice into a large mixing bowl. Add ⅓ cup of the sugar and mix together well.

>**3** In a separate bowl, beat together the egg whites. Add the margarine, yogurt, and vanilla extract and mix together well, then stir in the blueberries until thoroughly mixed.

>**4** Add the fruit mixture to the dry ingredients, then gently stir until just combined. Do not overstir—it is fine for it to be a little lumpy.

>5 Divide the batter evenly among the muffin cups to about two-thirds full. Mix the remaining sugar with the remaining allspice and sprinkle it over the muffins.

>6 Bake in the preheated oven for 25 minutes, or until well risen. Remove the muffins from the oven.

apricot, macadamia & white chocolate chunk muffins

makes 12 muffins

ingredients

2¼ cups all-purpose flour
1 tablespoon baking
  powder
½ cup granulated sugar
½ cup chopped dried
  apricots
⅓ cup chopped
  macadamia nuts
2 ounces white chocolate,
  chopped
2 eggs, beaten
1 cup buttermilk
½ cup sunflower oil

 1 Preheat the oven to 400°F. Place 12 muffin cups in a muffin pan or on a baking sheet.

 2 Sift the flour and baking powder into a bowl and stir in the sugar, apricots, nuts, and chocolate.

Serve the muffins warm, preferably on the day of making.

> **3** Beat together the eggs, buttermilk, and oil, then add to the bowl and stir to mix evenly.

> **4** Spoon the batter into the muffin cups and bake in the preheated oven for 20–25 minutes, until well risen.

rocky road bars

makes 8 bars

ingredients

6 ounces milk or semisweet
  dark chocolate

4 ounces butter

4 ounces shortcake cookies,
  broken into pieces

1½ cups miniature white
  marshmallows

½ cup walnuts or peanuts

confectioners' sugar, sifted,
  for dusting

>1 Line a 7-inch square cake pan with parchment paper.

>2 Break the chocolate into squares and place in a heatproof bowl.

>3 Set the bowl over a saucepan of gently simmering water and heat until the chocolate is melted, being careful to make sure that the bowl does not touch the water.

>4 Add the butter and stir until melted and combined. Let cool slightly.

>5 Stir the broken cookies, marshmallows, and nuts into the chocolate mixture.

>6 Pour the chocolate mixture into the lined pan, pressing down with the back of a spoon. Chill in the refrigerator for at least 2 hours, or until firm.

>7 Carefully invert onto a cutting board.

>8 Dust with confectioners' sugar.

Cut into eight pieces to serve.

chocolate chip cookies

makes 30 cookies

ingredients

1⅓ cups all-purpose flour
1 teaspoon baking powder
1 stick soft margarine, plus
  extra for greasing
⅓ cup light brown sugar
¼ cup granulated sugar
½ teaspoon vanilla extract
1 egg
¾ cup semisweet dark
  chocolate chips

>1 Preheat the oven to 375°F. Lightly grease and line two baking sheets.

>2 Place all of the ingredients in a large mixing bowl and beat until well combined.

Serve immediately or store in
an airtight container.

>3 Place tablespoonfuls of the dough on the
prepared baking sheets, spacing them well
apart to allow for spreading during cooking.

>4 Bake in the preheated oven for
10–12 minutes, or until the cookies
are golden brown. Using a spatula,
transfer the cookies to a wire rack to
cool completely.

almond biscotti

makes about 35

ingredients

1¾ cups whole blanched almonds

1⅔ cups all-purpose flour, plus extra for dusting

1 cup granulated sugar, plus extra for sprinkling

1 teaspoon baking powder

½ teaspoon ground cinnamon

2 eggs

2 teaspoons vanilla extract

>1 Preheat the oven to 350°F. Line two baking sheets with parchment paper.

 >2 Coarsely chop the almonds, leaving some whole.

>3 Mix together the flour, sugar, baking powder, and cinnamon in a mixing bowl. Stir in the almonds.

>4 Beat the eggs with the vanilla extract in a small bowl, then add to the flour mixture and mix together to form a firm dough.

>5 Invert the dough onto a lightly floured surface and knead lightly.

>6 Divide the dough in half and shape each piece into a log about 2 inches wide. Transfer to the prepared baking sheets and sprinkle with sugar. Bake in the preheated oven for 20–25 minutes, until firm.

>7 Remove from the oven and let cool slightly, then transfer to a cutting board and cut into ½-inch slices. Meanwhile, reduce the oven temperature to 325°F.

>8 Arrange the slices, cut side down, on the baking sheets. Bake in the oven for 15–20 minutes, until dry and crisp. Transfer to a wire rack to cool.

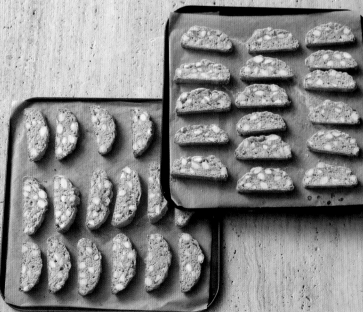

Store in an airtight container
to keep crisp.

crusty white bread

makes 1 loaf

ingredients
1 egg
1 egg yolk
⅔–1 cup lukewarm water

3⅔ cups white bread flour,
  sifted, plus extra for dusting
1½ teaspoons salt
2 teaspoons sugar

1 teaspoon active dry yeast
2 tablespoons butter, diced
oil, for greasing

>1 Place the egg and egg yolk in a liquid measuring cup and beat lightly to mix. Add enough water to make up to 1¼ cups. Stir well.

>2 Place the flour, salt, sugar, and yeast in a large bowl. Add the butter and rub it in with your fingertips until the mixture resembles fine bread crumbs.

>3 Make a well in the center, add the egg mixture, and work to a smooth dough. Invert onto a lightly floured surface and knead well for about 10 minutes, until smooth.

>4 Brush a bowl with oil. Shape the dough into a ball, place in the bowl, cover, and let rise in a warm place for 1 hour, or until doubled in volume.

>5 Preheat the oven to 425°F. Grease a 9-inch loaf pan. Invert the dough onto a lightly floured surface and knead for 1 minute until smooth.

>6 Shape the dough so it is the same length as the loaf pan and three times the width. Fold the dough in three widthwise and place it in the pan with the seam underneath.

>7 Cover and let rest in a warm place for 30 minutes, until the dough has risen above the pan.

>8 Place in the preheated oven and bake for 30 minutes, or until firm and golden brown. Transfer to a wire rack and let cool.

Cut into thick slices and serve.

pesto & olive soda bread

makes 1 loaf

ingredients
olive oil, for greasing
2 cups all-purpose flour
2 cups whole-wheat flour
1 teaspoon baking soda
½ teaspoon salt
3 tablespoons pesto
about 1¼ cups buttermilk,
½ cup coarsely chopped,
 pitted green olives
milk, for glazing

> **1** Preheat the oven to 400°F and line and grease a baking sheet. Sift the flours, baking soda, and salt into a bowl, adding back any bran from the sifter.

> **2** Mix together the pesto and buttermilk. Stir the mixture into the flour with the olives, mixing to a soft dough. Add more liquid, if needed.

Serve the soda bread on the day of baking.

> **>3** Shape the dough into an 8-inch circle and place on the baking sheet. Flatten slightly and cut a deep cross with a sharp knife.

> **>4** Brush with milk and bake in the preheated oven for 30–35 minutes, until golden brown. The loaf should sound hollow when tapped underneath.

scones

makes 9 scones

ingredients

3⅔ cups all-purpose flour,
  plus extra for dusting
½ teaspoon salt
2 teaspoons baking powder
4 tablespoons butter
2 tablespoons granulated
  sugar
1 cup milk, plus extra
  for glazing
strawberry preserves and
  crème fraîche, to serve

> **1** Preheat the oven to 425°F and line a baking sheet with parchment paper. Sift the flour, salt, and baking powder into a bowl. Rub in the butter using your fingertips until the mixture resembles fine bread crumbs.

> **2** Stir in the sugar. Make a well in the center and pour in the milk. Using a spatula, stir together to make a soft dough.

Serve freshly baked with strawberry preserves and créme fraîche.

>3 Invert the dough onto a lightly floured surface and lightly flatten until ½ inch thick. Cut out scones using a 2½-inch cookie cutter and place on the lined baking sheet.

>4 Brush with a little milk and bake in the preheated oven for 10–12 minutes, until golden and well risen. Let cool on a wire rack.

Index